UNACCUSTOMED AS I AM...

C. KENT WRIGHT

UNACCUSTOMED
AS I AM . . .

An Anthology
designed for
The After-Dinner Speaker

*

No man can make a fortune or a figure in this country without speaking, and speaking well, in public. *Lord Chesterfield*

What I crave first and foremost in an anthology is the pleasure of feasting on exquisite scraps, passages one relishes in a fresh sort of way because they are taken out of their context.
Desmond MacCarthy

That's not such a very long speech after all. At a public dinner they would hardly even call it a few remarks. *W. Somerset Maugham*

*

London
GEORGE ALLEN & UNWIN LTD
Ruskin House Museum Street

FIRST PUBLISHED IN 1950
SECOND IMPRESSION 1956

PRINTED IN GREAT BRITAIN
BY BRADFORD AND DICKENS
LONDON, W.C.1

To

JOHN RODGERS

who, as a member of Parliament,
cannot plead guilty to the title,

D. D. D.

. . . 'What, again?'

The *Hibbert Journal*

'Quelle délicatesse!'

Revue des deux Mondes

'O tempora! O mores!'

The *Tribuna* of Rome

'On n'a qu'à voir ce livre
pour vouloir le lire, et l'on
n'a que le lire pour vouloir
l'écarter'

Le Journal of Paris

Ἐὰν ζητῇς, καλῶς εὑρήσεις

M. Negrigepopolos, writing in

ὁ ἀγγελος (Athens)

INTRODUCTION

'It is a law of nature,' Sir Max Beerbohm once wrote, 'that no reviewer of an anthology can find *nothing* therein to carp at.'

This anthology will, I am sure, be no exception to that law. If it needs an excuse, I cannot think of a better one than to say that, in my view, no literary terrain has been so neglected by the anthologist as that of the aphorism and the epigram.

'The art of quotation,' wrote Disraeli, 'requires more delicacy in the practice than those conceive who can see nothing more in a quotation than an extract.' To excavate a sentence, which will stand and shine alone out of its context, is a task which not only calls for some discrimination and ingenuity, but which also satisfies the collector's instinct. It is, moreover, a pleasant hobby. It affords a salutary escape from the verbiage of Acts of Parliament and Statutory Instruments and the jargon of government circulars which form the background of my official life. (Though, I must confess, it is a hobby which brings no prestige in the home—my wife would much prefer that I took up carpentry or conjuring!). Of this anthology I can say with Montaigne, 'I have but gathered a nosegay of strange flowers and have put nothing of mine into it but the thread to bind them.'

To cut the world to pieces with an epigram is an ambition which stirs the hearts of many young men. At Oxford, I often wished to emulate Leslie Hore-Belisha, Tommy Earp and Beverley Nichols in amusing the Oxford Union with some brilliant and coruscating speech. But, in fact, it was usually somewhere about eleven o'clock that I succeeded in catching the speaker's eye, and my efforts at speech-making deserved, if they did not receive, the astringent comment in *The Isis*: 'Mr. . . . entertained doubts, but not his audience.' Though I hope that this anthology may be helpful to public speakers in general, it is primarily designed for the use of after-dinner speakers. The aphorisms, quotations and anecdotes which it contains may, perhaps, serve as pegs on which they can hang their own ideas, or; to vary the metaphor, may help them to 'strike a match on the seat of their intellectual pants.'

Whether they are replying for the guests, or speaking on behalf of the Wine and Food Society, the Marriage Guidance Council, the Gardeners' Guild, the Worshipful Company of Haberdashers, the Institute of Town Planning, the Noise Abatement League, or the Law Society, they will discover, I hope, something to quote or something upon which to elaborate.

There is one feature of this little book which may perhaps arouse criticism—the mixture of the serious and the flippant, the juxtaposition of gnomic wisdom and cynical levity. Such juxtapositions are deliberate. The book is meant to be a gallimaufry, and a gallimaufry it assuredly is.

As Mr. Rostrevor Hamilton has well said: 'To the reader, the epigram can give a varied delight; laughter, the relish of malice; a new insight, a moment of stillness and beauty won from sorrow; these and many other things; and in a few, a very few, cases, infinity in the palm of the hand.'

A FEW HINTS ON
AFTER-DINNER SPEAKING

Balaam's ass spoke well once, but it never tried it again. Altogether it differed greatly from its brethren. *C. H. Spurgeon*

To excel in the art of after-dinner speaking is a great social accomplishment. But, as in the world of letters easy reading means hard writing, so only the most expert after-dinner speakers can afford to speak without considerable preparation. The technique of social speaking is, in fact, deplorably neglected. Voltaire, in one of his letters from England, once remarked: 'The necessity of saying something, the perplexity of having nothing to say, and a desire of being witty, are three circumstances which alone are capable of making even the greatest writer ridiculous.' If that is true of a writer it applies with equal cogency to the speaker.

Consider the innumerable dinners, banquets and lunches which are enjoyed throughout this country in a year. Think of the countless conferences of institutes and technical associations, at each of which there is at least one official dinner and anything from six to a dozen after-dinner speeches. Alas! few of them remain in the memory for long after the function is over and very few rise above the level of mediocrity. The enjoyment which ought to be created by after-dinner speaking, this typically English institution of social intercourse, badinage and story-telling is so often marred simply because of the prevalent idea that '*anybody* can make an after-dinner speech.' Speaking after dinner is an art, and, like other arts, requires study, preparation and practice.

[ix]

The success of an after-dinner speech depends as much on the homeliness and informality of its delivery, as on its content. However large the gathering and however starched the shirts, the speaker should try to impart an atmosphere of cosy friendliness, as if he were speaking to a few of his own intimate friends round his own fireside. As Mr. Archibald Crawford, K.C., has well said in his book *Public Speaking*: 'The ideal for after-dinner speaking is the unfettered expression of one's personality relevantly to the subject-matter of the occasion. Let the beginner get hold of one or two amusing and, if he likes, fantastic ideas and talk to the audience in the most natural manner possible. After dinner is supremely the occasion for being simply yourself. . . . If you would only realize that an after-dinner audience is usually an indulgent one, asking nothing better than to be entertained, the fears that usually ruin after-dinner speaking would disappear.'

Here are some excellent hints for after-dinner speakers which were drawn up by the late Lord Bryce:

1. If you can find nothing at all to say, don't say it.

2. Always know what you mean to say.

3. Arrange your remarks in some sort of order.

4. At all hazards be clear.

   (Don't emulate the Bishop in the country church, who said: 'Nature herself shall be the palimpsest on which Omnipotence shall inscribe the character of a rejuvenated humanity.' Remember Emerson's maxim: 'Eloquence is the power to translate a truth into language perfectly intelligible to the person to whom you speak.'

5. Reflect on the kind of audience you are likely to have.

6. Never despise those whom you address.

7. Be sparing of literary ornament.

8. Beware of abusing humorous stories.

9. Never be dull. It is better to be flippant than to be dull.

To these might be added a few 'dont's.'

1. Don't profess undue modesty by saying that you have no idea why you were chosen to speak.

(It is much better to stand up boldly, cheekily if you like, and say, 'I can think of no one so suitable as I to propose this toast.')

2. Don't dawdle at the outset, but drive into your subject as quickly as possible.

3. Don't drag in a story unless it fully illustrates a point.

4. In the words of Oliver Wendell Holmes:
'Don't strew your pathway with those dreadful errs.'

5. Don't tell your audience that you will not speak for long. They won't believe you.

(I always distrust the speaker who begins: 'I am not going to make a speech BUT—' He is always good for at least twenty minutes.)

6. Don't in any circumstances read your speech, but speak from notes if you must. To sway an audience, you must watch them as you speak.

7. Don't introduce into your speech, religion,

serious politics, complaints, propaganda, *risqué* stories or apologies.

Above all, never be patronising, either to a respondent to the toast which you are proposing or to the company at large. Learn to shrink (or try to expand) to the intellectual stature of your audience. Be warned by the story of the young American who once found himself seated next to Mr. Wellington Koo at a diplomatic banquet. Completely at a loss as to what to say to a Chinese, this young man, with a touch of genius, such as may be detected only in those who are most adept in dropping their bricks with the most crashing thunder, said 'Likee soupee?' Mr. Koo smiled and nodded. A few minutes afterwards, when called on to say a few words, Mr. Koo delivered a brilliant talk in flawless English and sat down while the applause was still ringing. Turning to the young man, he said: 'Likee speechee?'

It is an admirable thing to introduce one or two stories, provided that they are apposite and not too well-known. To introduce a story by saying, 'That reminds me of . . .' or 'I heard a very good story' is bad. If you have an apt story, let it glide in of its own account by saying, 'Like the Aberdonian who . . .' or 'As happened in the case of the American on his first visit to Oxford . . .' In this way, the story becomes part of the speech, instead of remaining an interloper.

Let me give one example of an anecdotal aptness and one of rather grim banality. A friend of mine had to propose the toast of His Majesty's Ministers at a dinner where Sir Stafford Cripps was to have represented the Government. At the last moment, Sir Stafford found himself unable to attend and asked Mr. Douglas Jay to take his place. The proposer of the toast, who is a keen cross-word addict, said that he had been doing *The Times* cross-word and the clue for one word in the puzzle was 'What comes between I and K?' The solution was 'Popinjay' and that, he thought, was exactly what Sir Stafford had decided to do that evening.

Here, by way of contrast, is a short extract from a press report of a banquet held in the City of London. 'The Lord Mayor replied in witty manner and told a capital story concerning the Chairman of the evening. "Sir Blank," he said, "recently visited the South of France. When asked what he was doing there, his reply was that he proposed to undergo a slimming course, in order that he might become the dancing partner of Mae West." Roars of laughter, needless to say, greeted the joke.' The dinner—and the wines—must have been exceptionally good!

Among the masters of the art of after-dinner speaking whom I have had the privilege of hearing often was the late Mr. Ralph Strauss, who to the world at large was better known as a novelist, critic and amateur criminologist than as a public speaker. His method of making a speech illustrates what I have said earlier about the enormous effect which gesture, mannerisms and the form of delivery can have on the success of a speech. Mr. Strauss would hesitate, trail off his sentences into semi-incoherence or eloquent aposiopesis, wave his horn-rimmed spectacles or pull them down on to the tip of his nose, leave some fantastical, outrageous innuendo in mid-air, and would have no need to finish his sentence because he had got the minds of his audience running ahead of the spoken word. Even if he tried to finish his sentences, he would often be unable to do so, because of the gusts of uproarious laughter from his audiences. '*C'est une grande entreprise que celle de faire rire les honnêtes gens!* '

What is the appropriate *length* of after-dinner speeches? No hard and fast rule can, of course, be given. Joe Louis once said: 'After-dinner speeches should be like my second Schmelling fight and last about three seconds.' The length of speeches must vary according to the place of the speech on the toast list and the position held by the speaker. In either proposing or replying to the principal toast of the evening, it would perhaps be unwise to speak for less than fifteen minutes. On the other hand, where the toast of the guests appears near the end of the toast list, and there are two or more people down to reply for the guests, five minutes is certainly ample time for each reply. It is always preferable to err on the side of brevity. Where several people reply on behalf of the guests, how pleasant it would be if the second and third respondents were to imitate a Member of Parliament called Cruger who, at the conclusion of one of Burke's eloquent harangues, finding nothing to add, or perhaps as he thought to add with effect, exclaimed earnestly: 'I say *ditto* to Mr. Burke! I say *ditto* to Mr. Burke!!'

Remember the dangers of becoming intoxicated with the exuberance of your own verbosity. A Member of Parliament was called upon to reply for the visitors at one dinner. He apparently forgot where he was, and, after speaking for twenty minutes, remarked in a burst of eloquence: 'I not only speak for you, but I speak for generations yet unborn,' whereupon someone interjected: 'If you don't hurry up, they will be here before you've finished.' Mr. Bernard Shaw was once invited to speak at a dinner where the speeches had been far too many and far too long for the patience of the audience. They waited expectantly for Mr. Shaw, who was to speak last. When the roar of applause had subsided, 'Ladies and gentlemen,' he said, 'the subject is not exhausted, but we are,' and sat down.

Speakers should not be afraid of poking gentle fun at their audiences. If this is done good-humouredly, the audience, far from resenting it, will appreciate a good laugh against themselves. I remember once hearing the Marquess of Reading begin his reply on behalf of the guests at an annual dinner of the Chartered Surveyors Institution by saying that, until he had received the invitation, he did not know that there *was* such a creature as a Chartered Surveyor, as the only people with whom he associated the word 'chartered' were accountants and libertines. This quip delighted his audience and formed an admirable prelude to his subsequent speech, in which he paid serious tribute to the many-sided activities of the Institution.

There are some speakers—but very few—who can rely on past experience and practice to make an *impromptu* after-dinner speech. The late Lord Birkenhead was one of them. He was once the guest of honour at an annual dinner. He arrived late and whispered to one of the guests whom he knew. 'What is all this about?' He was told, 'It is the So-and-So Engineers.' 'Thank-you,' said Lord Birkenhead and proceeded to his place at the top table. When called upon to speak, he launched out into an obviously unprepared speech on engineering, science, mechanics, on energy, on concentration, on impulse and enthusiasm, so that no matter what might have been the calling of any listener present, he could without doubt consider these learned remarks to have been addressed to himself. At the end, he quoted Disraeli's dictum that 'No contingency can possibly occur, however fearful, however tremendous it may appear, from which a man by his own energy, may not extricate himself, as a mariner, by the rattling of his cannon can dissipate the impending waterspout.' This peroration evoked a positive *furore* of applause, during which Lord Birkenhead left the restaurant to fulfil ' another engagement.' The friend of whom he had inquired the nature and purpose of the dinner met him later in the evening in the card room of an adjacent club. Lord Birkenhead turned his head from his cards and said: 'By the way, *who* did you say those people were to whom I spoke to-night?'

At a recent meeting of the Hampstead Parliament, Lord Reading offered this golden rule for after-dinner speakers—'Always be shorter than anybody dared to hope.' Other suggestions which he made were:

That long-winded speakers should be made to wear an L-plate in their button-holes;

That coupons should be issued for every 1,000 words, with 'supplementaries';

It should, moreover, be an offence (a) to speak under the influence of alcohol, (b) to exceed the time limit, (c) to speak to the public danger.

Much depends on a good beginning of a speech. A classic example of a witty opening sentence, which plunges at once *in medias res* is that of Professor A. E. Housman. Speaking at a dinner at Trinity College, Cambridge, he began: 'Gentlemen, this Hall has seen Wordsworth drunk and Porson sober, and I, who am a greater scholar than Wordsworth

and a greater poet then Porson, now stand here—
betwixt and between.'

What then, are the essentials of a good after-dinner
speech? It should be topical, tactful and not too long.
It should be a happy mixture of seriousness and levity.
Begin on a light note and work up to a serious peroration. Success in after-dinner speaking means language
rightly chosen, a leavening of wit or humour, an
orderly arrangement of one's subject matter, an
effective and pleasing delivery, and an almost inde-
finable sense of the significance of emphasis. Para-
doxically enough, a good speech should *sound* impromptu, and much careful preparation is necessary
to achieve that effect. If a speech is learned by heart
and recited, it is in danger of sounding flat and
unconvincing. It is a rare experience to feel that you
have 'really brought the house down' with an after-
dinner speech, to have made your audience amused,
interested, expectant, eager for you to go on speaking.
If you do experience such a triumph, you will feel
amply rewarded for any amount of preparation and
rehearsal.

INDEX

✱

ON ARGUMENT

There are three sides to every question; your side, his side, and to hell with it. *Anon*

Every argument between two people is likely to sink or rise to the level of a dog-fight. *A. A. Milne*

When you convert someone to an idea . . . you lose your faith in it. *Oscar Wilde*

The sincere controversialist is above all things a good listener. *G. K. Chesterton*

'My husband never argues with me. He just says: "I have spoken".' *Woman at Police Court*

You have not converted a man because you have silenced him. *Lord Morley*

The Socratic manner is not a game at which two can play. *Sir Max Beerbohm*

The difference between a conviction and a prejudice is that you can explain a conviction without getting angry. *Anon*

The argument we had was to my liking. It lasted for hours. *Wife in Police Court*

The person who hasn't a leg to stand on is usually the one who does the most kicking. *Anon*

There are two sides to every question—the wrong side and our side. *American Proverb*

Our Disputants put me in mind of the Skuttle Fish, that when he is unable to extricate himself, blackens all the water about him, till he becomes invisible.
Joseph Addison

Never argue; repeat your assertion. *Robert Owen*

There is no arguing with him, for if his pistol misses fire, he knocks you down with the butt-end of it.
Oliver Goldsmith (of Dr. Johnson)

I never make the mistake of arguing with people for whose opinions I have no respect. *Edward Gibbon*

If you are dealing with a fool, dictate, but never argue, for you will lose your labour and perhaps your temper. *Oliver Wendell Holmes*

Answer not a fool according to his folly, lest thou also be like unto him. Answer a fool according to his folly lest he be wise in his own conceit. *Proverbs*

A man can't argue with the woman he loves. *Anon.*

Never ascribe to your opponent motives meaner than your own. *J. M. Barrie*

Talk often, but never long: in that case, if you do not please, at least you are sure not to tire your hearers. *Lord Chesterfield*

ON ART

Art does affect the lives of men; it moves to ecstasy, thus giving colour and movement to what might be otherwise a rather grey and trivial affair. Art for some makes life worth living. *Clive Bell*

Trees are trees and mountains are mountains to all of us. We can all put the same labels on things. But it is what we feel that matters. And that's where the fun begins. *Hervey Adams*

One reassuring thing about modern art is that things can't be as bad as they are painted. *M. Walthall Jackson*

Art is the expression of something one has seen which is bigger than oneself. *Oliver La Farge*

In the highest sense, a work of art is the expression of an emotional experience in some medium—stone, bronze, paint, words, or musical tone—in such a way that it may be transferred to other people.

F. E. Halliday

Art is most simply and most effectively defined as an attempt to create pleasing forms. Such forms satisfy our sense of beauty, and the sense of beauty is satisfied when we are able to appreciate a unity or harmony of formal relations among our sense-perceptions.

Herbert Read

Art is that imaginative expression of human energy which, through technical concretion of feeling and perception, tends to reconcile the individual with the universal by exciting in him impersonal emotion. And the greatest art is that which excites the greatest impersonal emotion in an hypothecated perfect human being. *John Galsworthy*

Art is a human activity consisting of this, that one man, usually by means of external signs, hands on to others feelings he has lived through, and that other people are infected by these feelings, and also experience them. *Tolstoy*

Self-complacency is the death of the artist.
W. Somerset Maugham

Art is the communication of total experience, science of abstracted experience. Art is synthetic, or, if you prefer it, preservative—it transmits a given moment of experience intact. Science is analytic.
Alex Comfort

Art is skill, that is the first meaning of the word. That meaning underlies all others. *Eric Gill*

Art, all art, has this characteristic that it unites people. *Tolstoy*

A true artist takes no notice whatever of the public.
Oscar Wilde

Poetry is the language in which man explores his own amazement. *Christopher Fry*

Somehow or other he blundered into magnificence. *Anon* (about the architect of All Souls College, Oxford.)

My tutor does watercolours; they are like the work of a girl of fourteen when she was twelve. *Ben Nicholson*

Shops and machines and factories will themselves become works of art, the moment man puts his soul into them, and not only his greed. *J. E. Barton*

But it is only in degenerate ages that the artist has been viewed as a conjuror who deceives the eye by inventing exact outward copies of nature in marble or paint. *Ibid*

Only the auctioneer should attempt to appreciate all schools of art. *Oscar Wilde*

It has been said that 'art is a tryst,' for in the joy of it maker and beholder meet. *Kojiro Tomita*

Alone of men—though with the farmer, the gardener and the sailor following him at a distance— the artist exercises a profession that is entirely beneficial, and creative in itself. He unlocks for others the gates of the mind, the senses and the soul.

Sir Osbert Sitwell

We go about the world purblind; and we can for the most part see only what has been pointed out to us; it is the poet's part to reveal new beauties, and thus, though infinitesimally, to increase the power of vision.

Alan Porter

B   [25]

ON THE ATOM

The atomic bomb is here to stay. But are we? *Anon*

> Who sees with equal eye, as God of all,
> A hero perish, or a sparrow fall,
> Atoms or systems into ruin hurled,
> And now a bubble bursts, and now a world.
> *Alexander Pope*

Finally, like the sorcerer's apprentice, we may practise our magic without knowing how to stop it, thus fulfilling the prophecy of Prospero. In view of our behaviour recently, I cannot pretend to deprecate such a possibility; but I think it is worth mentioning.
Bernard Shaw

The energy released by the scientists from the atomic bomb is almost paltry when compared with the human energy nullified and rendered useless by the order of the planners. *Sir Ernest Benn*

You may call it the accidental and fortuitous concourse of atoms.
(Of the combination of parties led by Mr. Disraeli and Mr. Gladstone, which defeated the Government on the Chinese War, March 5, 1857.)

The discovery of the atomic bomb has made men all the world over recognize the urgency of international organization more than anything else has done.
Lord Lindsay

Nearly fifty songs about atomic energy have now been copyrighted in the U.S.A., including Atom Bounce, Atom Boogie, and Up and At 'Em With Our Atom. But songs about love still lead.

Evening Standard

The last paradox—the split atom that unites the world—anyway what's left of it. *John A. Lincoln*

Does any thoughtful man suppose that the present experiment in civilisation is the last the world will see? *George Santayane*

> Let not the atom bomb
> Be the final sequel—
> In which all men—
> Are cremated equal.
>
> *Kaye Phelps*

Investors in oil, gas and coal power need not worry. Atomic power is not lying in wait to slug them around any corner they will turn in the near future.

Cuthbert Daniel and *Arthur M. Squires*

. . . "the intimate conviction that anything may happen, anything may be discovered—another war, the artificial creation of life, the proof of continued existence after death—why, it's all infinitely exhilarating.'

'And the possibility that everything may be destroyed?' questioned Mr. Carden.

'That's exhilarating too,' Calamy answered smiling.

Mr. Carden shook his head. 'It may be rather tame of me,' he said, 'but I confess, I prefer a more quiet life.' *Aldous Huxley*

Cheer up, the worst is yet to come.

Philander Chase Johnson

Man . . . like an angry ape
Plays such fantastic tricks before high heaven
As makes the angels weep . . .

Shakespeare

The scientists split the atom—and now the atom is splitting us. *Quentin Reynolds*

Nations that split hairs shouldn't split atoms.

John A. Lincoln

ON CHILDREN

Children are horribly insecure. The life of a parent is the life of a gambler. *Sydney Smith*

> How like an angel came I down!
> How bright were all things here!
> When first among his works I did appear.
> *Thomas Traherne*

Happy those early days when I shined in my angel infancy, before I understood this place. *Henry Vaughan*

All nurseries were the darkened scene of temporal oppression, fitfully lighted with the gaunt reflections of hell-fire. *Sir Max Beerbohm* (of a Victorian childhood)

Children are given to us to discourage our better emotions. *Saki*

Children are natural mimics—they act like their parents in spite of every attempt to teach them good manners. *Anon*

> She was not really bad at heart,
> But only rather rude and wild,
> She was an aggravating child.
> *Hilaire Belloc*

I was much distressed by the next-door people who had twin babies and played the violin; but one of the twins died and the other has eaten the fiddle, so all is peace. *Edward Lear*

[29]

None of the teachers ever raised his voice. None of the children ever lowered his, except through hoarseness. *Emily Hahn* (of a progressive school)

Reasoning with a child is fine, if you can reach the child's reason without destroying your own.

John Mason Brown

> The child that is not clean and neat
> With lots of toys and things to eat,
> He is a naughty child, I'm sure—
> Or else his dear papa is poor.

R. L. Stevenson

A happy childhood is one of the best gifts that parents have it in their power to bestow.

Mary Cholmondeley

The art of being a parent consists of sleeping when the baby isn't looking. *Anon*

How long does a boy really belong to you? Five, maybe six years. Then for ten years he is a savage, and for the next five years a callow introvert with mental growing pains. *Hal Boyle*

Child (reciting the Golden Rule): 'Do unto others before they do unto you.'

> O'er the rugged mountain's brow
>   Clara threw the twins she nursed,
> And remarked, 'I wonder now
>   Which will reach the bottom first.'

Harry Graham

[30]

By the time the youngest children have learned to keep the house tidy, the oldest grandchildren are on hand to tear it to pieces again. *Christopher Morley*

'I'm sorry to do this,' said a little boy, as he spread jam on his baby sister's face, 'but I can't have suspicion pointing its ugly finger at me.'

Parents used to strike children to discipline them. Now it is usually in self-defence. *Anon*

It may be bad for the child to give it a swift smack occasionally, but what a good thing it is for the mother! *Nursery World*

Never strike a child unless in anger—and then strike to kill. *Bernard Shaw*

It now costs more to amuse a child than it once did to educate his father. *Vaughan Monroe*

Children are a great comfort in your old age—and they help you to reach it faster, too. *Lionel M. Kaufman*

Small boy: 'If I'm noisy they give me a spanking . . . and if I'm quiet they take my temperature.' *Coronet*

Nothing offends children more than to play down to them. All the great children's books—the Pilgrim's Progress, Robinsoe Crusoe, Grimm's Fairy Tales and Gulliver's Travels—were written for adults.

Bernard Shaw

A lady's announcement to her girl-friends that she is going to do what, after all, quite a number of other women have done before—namely, give birth to a child—is the signal for them all to burst into tears.
Cornelia Otis Skinner

Children begin by loving their parents; as they grow older they judge them; sometimes they forgive them. *Oscar Wilde*

It is true that children are expensive, time-consuming, patience-taxing additions to the family, but the sacrifices they demand are trivial to what they give. *Chad Walsh*

Children often hold a marriage together—by keeping their parents too busy to quarrel with each other. *The Saturday Evening Post*

It agreeth not with reason that a child be alwaies muzzled, cockered, dandled and brought up in his parents' lap or sight; for so much as their natural kindnesse, or, as I might call it, tender fondnesse, causeth often, even the wisest to prove so idle, so overnice, and so base-minded. *Montaigne*

ON CLOTHES

Women who are not vain about their clothes are often vain about not being vain about their clothes. *Cyril Scott*

> Dorttur, seyde the good wyfe,
>   hyde thy legys whyte,
> And schew not forth thy stret hossyn
>   to make men have de-lytt.
>   *Anon* (15th century)

. . . Those weird, hieroglyphic bursts of Neon lighting, sagging naïvely over their trousers like an Egyptian holiday. . . . Description of American men's shirtings in the *Tailor & Cutter*.

She well knew the great architectural secret of decorating her constructions and never descended to construct a decoration. *Anthony Trollope*

Fashion is gentility running away from vulgarity, and afraid of being overtaken. *William Hazlitt*

A man that likes women's hats is either a fool or a pervert. A hat's the one thing women buy to arouse other women's envy. *James S. Pollack*

However extravagant or bizarre, 'male costume never jests.' No shop assistant ever sold a man a hat by presenting it as 'amusing.' *Margaret Lane*

[33]

. . . the lady who declared 'that the sense of being perfectly dressed gives a feeling of inward tranquillity which religion is powerless to bestow.' *R. W. Emerson*

. . . she has this new dress with poppies all over it, it is like Carter's Tested Seeds. ' It is called Every One Came Up. *Stevie Smith*

The new long skirts are truly bliss
To girls with legs like this ( ) or this) (.

Anon

Never be the first nor the last in the fashion.
Lord Chesterfield

She wears her clothes as if they were thrown on her with a pitchfork. *Dean Swift*

The art of dress is always alive, for the simple reason that no smart woman in any civilized age has ever consented to wear anything that is even six months out of date. *J. E. Barton*

A visit to a country house is a series of meals mitigated by the new dresses of the ladies. *Benjamin Disraeli*

What would we say if men changed the length of their trousers every year? *Lady Astor*

Any man may be in good spirits and good temper when he's well dressed. There ain't much credit in that. *Charles Dickens*

ON COMMITTEES

If Moses had been a Committee, the Israelites would still be in Egypt. *J. B. Hughes*

Nothing is ever accomplished by a Committee unless it consists of three members, one of whom happens to be sick and the other absent. *Hendrik van Loon*

Another reaction of the novice may be that Committee routine—reading of minutes, passing resolutions—savour of defunct etiquette: It could all be settled by a little 'friendly chat!' *Kay Gilmour*

> Lord Lilac thought it rather rotten
> That Shakespeare should be quite forgotten,
> And, therefore, got on a Committee
> With several chaps out of the City.
> $\qquad$ *G. K. Chesterton*

A Committee is a group of men who, individually, can do nothing, but collectively can meet and decide that nothing can be done. *Anon*

The Committee is one of man's important social discoveries—like the use of money, the rule of law and the specialisation of labour—but it is not a panacea. To solve problems, it is not enough merely to set up Committees. They can moderate and guide the creative energy of individual men, but they can never be a substitute for it. *Anthony Ashton*

[35]

It is a thousand pities
And one of the worst of menaces
That all committees
   —By a sort of parthenogenesis—

Almost at once and as if to prove their worth
And quite impervious to snubs
Give birth
To not less than four little subs.

Wherefore I have sometimes thought
That it might be very nice
If each newly formed committee could be caught
In time, and fitted with a suitable contraceptive
   device.

Dr. L. N. Jackson in *The Lancet*

. . . the State, that cawing rookery of committees
and sub-committees. *V. S. Pritchett*

He murmured, as he left the Conference table,
'How tranquil must have been the Tower of Babel!'

Anon

A committee is a *cul de sac* to which ideas are lured
and then quietly strangled. *John A. Lincoln*

ON CONSCIENCE

I have a terrible conscience—it doesn't keep me from doing things; it just keeps me from enjoying them.

New York Journal American

Knowledge without conscience is but the ruine of soule. *Rabelais*

Some certain dregs of conscience are yet within me.

Shakespeare (Henry VIII)

A man has less conscience when in love than in any other condition. *Schopenhauer*

Ah, what an embarrassment is a conscience, and how happy one might be if one were without it! *E. Augier*

A man's conscience and his judgment is the same thing, and, as the judgment, so also the conscience may be erroneous. *Hobbes (Leviathan)*

What saith thy conscience? 'Thou shalt become what thou art.' *Nietzsche*

Conscience—the thing that aches when everything is feeling good. *Anon*

Conscience. The power of it is well indicated by that statement of John Henry Newman, in a note to the Apologia, that men 'would rather be in error with the sanction of their conscience, than be right with the mere judgment of their reason.'

W. Somerset Maugham

[37]

ON COURTSHIP & MARRIAGE

The pleasantest part of a man's life is generally that which passes in courtship, provided his passion be sincere and the party beloved kind with discretion. *Addison*

Oh, my young friends, how delightful is the beginning of a love business, and how undignified sometimes the end. *William Makepeace Thackeray*

Love is the most subtle form of self-interest. *Holbrook Jackson*

We cannot live by Freud alone. *Christopher Fry*

Between a woman's 'Yes' and 'Nay' I would not engage to put a pin's point, so close they be to one another. *Cervantes*

I do not like the sort of person at all; the sort of person I like is a modest woman, who stays at home and looks after her husband's dinner.
Thomas Love Peacock

He married an Anglo-Indian widow, and soon after published a pamphlet in favour of suttee.
George Meredith

Marriage is not like the hill Olympus, wholly clear, without clouds; yea, expect both wind and storm sometimes, which, when blown over, the air is clearer and wholesomer for it. *Thomas Fuller*

Love in marriage cannot live nor subscribe unless it be mutual; and where love cannot be, there can be left of wedlock nothing but the empty husk of an outside matrimony, as undelightful and unpleasing to God as any other kind of hypocrisy. *John Milton*

They that have grown old in a single state are generally found to be morose, fretful and captious.
Dr. Johnson

. . . for very soon a beautiful smile would light up a round, rosy, very ordinary face, suffusing it, transforming a plain woman into one to whose one's heart gave unstintingly, convinced that all that is necessary to be happy is to be with her. *George Moore*

Is not marriage an open question, when it is alleged, from the beginning of the world, that such as are in the institution want to get out; and such as are out want to get in. *R. W. Emerson*

Marriage is the great puzzle of our day. It is our Sphinx-riddle. Solve it, or be torn to bits, is the decree. *D. H. Lawrence*

It is human, when we do not understand another human being, and cannot ignore him, to exert an unconscious pressure on that person to turn him into something that we *can* understand: many husbands and wives exert this pressure on each other.
T. S. Eliot

A fat woman is a quilt for the winter.
Punjabi Proverb

Marriage, which makes two one, is a lifelong struggle to discover which is that one. *Anon*

Men may have rounded Seraglio Point; they have not yet doubled Cape Turk. *George Meredith*

I expect that woman will be the last thing civilised by man. *Ibid*

The worst reconciliation is preferable to the best divorce. *Cervantes*

Marriage is a noose, which, fastened about the neck, runs the closer and fits more uneasy by our struggling to get loose: it is a Gordian knot which none can untie, and, being twisted with our thread of life, nothing but the scythe of death can sever it. *Ibid*

Marriage is the earliest fruit of civilisation and it will be the latest. I think a man and a woman should choose each other for life, for the simple reason that a long life with all its accidents is barely long enough for a man and a woman to understand each other; and in this case to understand is to love. The man who understands one woman is qualified to understand pretty well anything. *John Butler Yeats*

His wife might not be a clever woman, but she was a cosy woman, and there was a lot to be said for cosiness in this very uncosy world. *J. B. Priestley*

Some modern pathologists hold that love is an intoxication of the nervous system. *Anon*

On the way to Aarhus, I saw a very comical sight. Two cows, which were tied together, cantered past us; the one was gaddish, and had a swing of genius about its tail; the other, as it appeared, was more prosaic, and was depressed at having to take part in the same movements. Do not most marriages turn out to be like that? *Søren Kierkegaard*

My husband will never chase another woman. He's too fine, too decent, too old. *Gracie Allen*

The most difficult year of marriage is the one you're in. *Franklin P. Jones*

My wife and I had words—but I never got to use mine. *Fibber McGee*

'He was a comedian on the stage,' said the wife of a celebrated "funny" man, 'but a tragedian in the home.' *W. Macneile Dixon*

It is no excuse if you are neglecting your wife to say it doesn't matter because she is only a relation by marriage. *Sir Seymour Hicks*

Without women we should all be reasonable, Edward; there would be no instinct, and a reasonable world—what would it be like? A garden without flowers, music without melody. *George Moore*

More hearts are severed in the kitchen than were ever united at the altar. *Russell Green*

'He gradually wormed his way out of my confidence.' *Nunnally Johnson*

Were it not for imagination, sir, a man would be as happy in the arms of a chambermaid as of a Duchess.
Dr. Johnson

No sane woman ever loved a man before she knew him. Did any sane woman afterward? *Anon*

If you can make a woman laugh she's nearly yours: if you can make her cry, you'll wish she wasn't.
Sir Seymour Hicks

A lover who reasons is no lover. *Norman Douglas*

If a woman has had more than three husbands, she poisons them; avoid her. *William Maguire*

A wise woman will always let her husband have her way. *R. B. Sheridan*

There is always one woman who teaches a man everything. *Anon*

All sentimentalists are criminals. *Norman Douglas*

The great secret of successful marriage is to treat all disasters as incidents and none of the incidents as disasters. *Harold Nicolson*

Overheard: 'I married her because we have so many faults in common.'

The greatest charm of marriage, in fact that which renders it irresistible to those who have once tasted it, is the duologue, the permanent conversation between two people which talks over everything and everyone till death breaks the record. *Cyril Connolly*

Strange to say what delight we married people have to see these poor fools decoyed into our condition. *Samuel Pepys*

That is the nature of women, not to love when we love them, and to love when we love them not. *Cervantes*

The only trouble about being able to read a woman like a book is that you're liable to forget your place. *Anon*

If you wish women to love you, be original; I know a man who used to wear felt boots summer and winter, and women fell in love with him. *Tchekhov*

A wife is to thank God her Husband hath faults . . . A Husband without faults is a dangerous observer. *Lord Halifax*

Marriage is one long conversation, chequered by disputes. *R. L. Stevenson*

A perfect marriage is a hearth and a horizon. *Princess Antoine Bibesco*

To marry is to get a binocular view of life. *Rev. W. R. Inge*

[43]

It destroys one's nerves to be amiable every day to the same human being. *Benjamin Disraeli*

As the faculty of writing has been chiefly a masculine endowment, the reproach of making the world miserable has been always thrown upon the woman.

Dr. Johnson

He[1] had the supreme character of the domestic despot—that his good temper was, if possible, more despotic than his bad temper. *G. K. Chesterton*

Love lives on propinquity and dies of contact.

Thomas Hardy

I often think that women, even those who think themselves experienced in sexual strategy, do not know how to manage an honest man. *Ibid*

Mr. Bennet treated the matter differently. 'So, Lizzy,' said he one day, 'your sister is crossed in love, I find. I congratulate her. Next to being married, a girl likes to be crossed in love a little now and then. It is something to think of, and gives her a sort of distinction among her companions.' *Jane Austen*

I should like to see any kind of a man, distinguishable from a gorilla, that some good and even pretty woman could not shape a husband out of.

Oliver Wendell Holmes

Marriage has many pains, but celibacy has no pleasures. *Dr. Johnson*

[1] Charles Dickens.

ON DEFINITIONS

History is a pattern of timeless moments. *T. S. Eliot*

War is mainly a catalogue of blunders.
Winston Churchill

Opinion Surveys: people who don't matter reporting on opinions that do matter. *John A. Lincoln.*

Bank: an institution which will lend you money if you can prove that you do not need it. *Anon*

Worry is interest paid on trouble before it is due. *Dr. W. R. Inge*

A recession is a period in which you tighten up your belt. In a depression you have no belt to tighten up— and when you have no pants to hold up, it's a panic. *Anon*

Failure is the path of least persistence. *Anon*

An extravagance is anything you buy that is of no earthly use to your wife. *Franklin P. Jones*

Gossip is the art of saying nothing in a way that leaves practically nothing unsaid. *Walter Winchell*

Scandal is gossip made tedious by morality.
Oscar Wilde

[45]

An epigram is striking a verbal match on the seat of your intellectual pants. *John A. Lincoln*

A professor is a man whose job it is to tell students how to solve the problems of life which he himself has tried to avoid by becoming a professor. *Anon*

A smart girl is one who can refuse a kiss without being deprived of it. *Anon*

Budget: A mathematical confirmation of your suspicions. *A. A. Latimer*

Civilisation is an active deposit which is formed by the combustion of the Present with the Past.
Cyril Connolly

A bachelor is one who thinks one can live as cheap as two. *Eleanor S. J. Ridley*

Tact: the ability to describe others as they see themselves. *Abraham Lincoln*

Consult: To seek another's approval of a course already decided on. *Ambrose Bierce*

Cynicism: the anticipation of the historical perspective. *Russell Green*

Cynic: a man who looks both ways before crossing a one-way street. *Anon*

Talking is the disease of age. *Ben Jonson*

[46]

Tree: an object that will stand in one place for years, then jump in front of a lady driver. *Ruth Lemezis*

Genius is a perception of the obvious which nobody else sees. *Anon*

Taste is the feminine of genius. *Edward FitzGerald*

Public Interest: term used by every politician to support his ideas. *W. M. Kiplinger*

Peace: a period of cheating between two periods of fighting. *Ambrose Bierce*

Philosophy: a route of many roads leading from nowhere to nothing. *Ibid*

Patience: a minor form of despair disguised as a virtue. *Ibid*

Pique is the spur the devil rides the noblest tempers with. *Sir George Savile*

Tolerance: another word for indifference.
W. Somerset Maugham

Television: radio with eyestrain.

Psychologist: a man who, when a beautiful girl enters the room, watches everybody else.
Bruce Patterson

Anatomy: something which we all have—but it looks a lot better on a girl. *Bruce Raeburn*

[47]

Bargain: something you can't use at a price you can't resist. *Franklin P. Jones*

Dancing is the art of pulling your feet away faster than your partner can step on them. *Anon*

Grandmother: an old lady who keeps your mother from spanking you.

Estate Agent: the man who puts you on his wailing list.

Meteorology: the science of being up in the air and all at sea. *E. L. Hawke*

I believe that genius is an infinite capacity for taking life by the scruff of the neck. *Christopher Quill*

Etiquette is learning to yawn with your mouth closed.
Anon

Conceit: God's gift to little men. *Bruce Barton*

Capitalist: one who lives on the wealth of brains— his father's or his own. *Anon*

A luxury: anything a husband needs. *Anon*

Hobby: a hard job of work you wouldn't do for a living. *Anon*

Celebrity: a man who works all his life to become famous enough to be recognised—then goes around in dark glasses so no one will know who he is.
Earl Wilson

Admiration: Our polite recognition of another, resemblance to ourselves. *Ambrose Bierce*

Success: (1) self-expression at a profit.
    (2) making more money to meet obligations you wouldn't have if you didn't have so much money. *Anon*
    (3) the ability to hitch your waggon to a star while keeping your feet on the ground. *Marcelene Cox*

Insomnia: a contagious disease often transmitted from babies to parents. *Shannon Fife*

Bore: (1) a man who deprives you of solitude without providing you with company.
                               Gian Vincenzo Gravina
(2) a man who, when you ask him how he is, tells you. *Anon*

(3) A person who talks when you wish him to listen.
                               Ambrose Bierce

An epigram is truth on a 'binge.' *John A. Lincoln.*

Fastidiousness is the ability to resist a temptation in the hope that a better one will come along. *Ibid*

Courage is not simply *one* of the virtues but the form of every virtue at the testing point, which means at the point of highest reality. *C. S. Lewis*

ON DIPLOMACY

Diplomacy is the art of letting someone have your way.
Daniele Varè

Some were known to scoff when he (Lord Grey of Falloden) spoke on an interview with an ambassador as of less importance than an appointment with a wild duck. *G. M. Trevelyan*

A diplomat is useful not only for what he does, but for what he is. Prestige is not action but irradiation.
Daniele Varè

To his ambassador in Warsaw, Napoleon gave the following instructions: 'Tenez bonne table et soignez les femmes.' In this, the New Diplomacy has brought no change. *Daniele Varè*

An ambassador is an honest man sent to lie abroad for the commonwealth. *Sir Henry Wotton*

All sceptres are crooked atop. *Francis Bacon*

Diplomacy—the business of handling a porcupine without disturbing the quills. *Anon*

Diplomacy is the ability to take something and make the other fellow believe he is giving it away.
Anon

ON DRINK

Every child born into the world opens its mouth to shout for a drink before it opens its eyes to see. It shouts for a drink and it gets one. It becomes a habit.
André L. Simon

The Persians are very fond of wine . . . It is also their general practice to deliberate upon affairs of weight when they are drunk; and that on the morning, when they are sober, the decision to which they came the night before is put before them by the master of the house in which it was made; and if it is then approved they act on it; if not, they set it aside. Sometimes, however, they are sober at their first deliberations, but in this case they always reconsider the matter under the influence of wine. *Herodotus*

The Persians were wise to discuss everything twice, once drunk at night and again sober in the morning. But in what state did they make the final decision?
Robin Smyth

Drunk for a 1d.
Dead drunk for 2d.
Clean straw for nothing.
Sign at a Southwark Inn. 18th Century

Eloquence is what you think you have after five Martinis. *Anon*

'What shall we drink?'
'Whatever you please—only let it be champagne.'
Tolstoy

Sir, I do not say it is wrong to produce self-complacency by drinking; I only deny that it improves the mind. *Dr. Johnson*

'I rather like bad wine,' said Mr. Mountchesney, 'one gets so bored with good wine.' *Benjamin Disraeli*

A new Japanese drink comprises sake (rice wine), alcohol, grape sugar, and lactic acid. 'It is a very democratic beverage,' says the head of the Tokio brewery. 'It makes all drinkers equal. Everybody—high and humble alike—falls down after drinking three glasses.'

'Champagne certainly gives one werry gentlemanly ideas, but for a continuance I don't know but I should prefer mild hale.' *R. S. Surtees*

ON ECONOMY

Beware of little expenses; a small leak will sink a great ship. *Benjamin Franklin*

No man is rich whose expenditure exceeds his means; and no one is poor whose income exceeds his outgoings. *Haliburton*

Buy not what you want but what you have need of, what you do not want is dear at a farthing. *Cato*

To-day's economic problem is to prevent our elastic currency from becoming just a stretch of the imagination. *Pathfinder Magazine, U.S.A.*

Statistics are castrated facts. *John A. Lincoln*

More and more these days I find myself pondering on how to reconcile my net income with my gross habits. *John Kirk Nelson*

> John Stuart Mill:
> By a mighty effort of will,
> Overcame his natural bonhomie,
> And wrote 'Principles of
>   Political Economy.'
>
> *E. C. Bentley*

There is no economy in going to bed early to save candles if the result be twins. *Chinese Proverb*

The outcome of the income depends on the outgo for the upkeep. *Anon*

[53]

ON EGOTISTS & EGOTISM

Nothing is so interesting as egotism when a man has an ego. *Frank Harris*

It is not what they think of me that matters, but what I think of them. *Queen Victoria*

An egotist is a man who thinks that a woman will marry him for himself alone. *Anon*

The surest way to be cheated is to think oneself cleverer than other people. *La Rochefoucauld*

You never say a word of yourself, dear Lady Grey. You have that dreadful sin of anti-egotism.
Sydney Smith

In the book of Egoism, it is written, Possession without obligation to the object possessed approaches felicity. *George Meredith*

Egoist: A person of low taste, more interested in himself than in me. *Ambrose Bierce*

Whereas it had been supposed that the fullest possible enjoyment is to be found in extending our ego to infinity, the truth is that the fullest possible enjoyment is to be found in reducing our ego to zero.
G. K. Chesterton

[54]

Yet egotism is good talk. Even dull biographers are pleasant to read; and if to read, why not to hear? *Thackeray*

A wife encourages her husband's egoism in order to exercise her own. *Russell Green*

Intolerance itself is a form of egoism, and to condemn egoism intolerantly is to share it. *George Santayana*

Take egotism out and you would castrate the benefactors. *R. W. Emerson*

'Really, when other people *will* talk, conversation becomes impossible.' *Anon* (quo. Desmond MacCarthy)

After the wedding: 'They should be very happy. They're both so in love with him.'

ON THE ENGLISH

We like to take ourselves for granted.

Sir Ernest Barker

What governs the Englishman is the inner atmosphere—the weather in his soul. *Prof. Santayana*

The English are the most interesting study in the world. I could write a book in worship of them, and another book damning them. *Walter H. Page*

We Englishmen have a habit of catching continental diseases in a milder form. *H. Maurice Rilton*

Any Englishman who is laughed at thinks it's because his tie is crooked. *'Beachcomber'*

An Englishman is a man who has never been able to tell a lie about others and who is never willing to face the truth about himself. *Michael Arlen*

The people of France have made it no secret that those of England, as a general thing, are, to their perception, an inexpressive and speechless race, perpendicular and unsociable, unaddicted to enriching any bareness of contact with verbal or other embroidery. *Henry James*

One of the characteristics of the English people is a certain complacent candour about their own most obvious defects. *Lady Violet Bonham Carter*

[56]

Of all the nations in the world at present, the English are the stupidest in speech, the wisest in action. *Carlyle*

How hard it is to make an Englishman acknowledge that he is happy. *Thackeray*

Those were the days when an Englishman's home was still to some extent his castle, not as now when every spinster is wont to look under her bed for an Enforcement Officer. *J. K. Stanford*

Among the qualities fused in the English character are common sense, an individualism which here degenerates into eccentricity and there is elevated into heroism, a desire to find salvation in the light cast by religion or art or science, and a capacity for enjoyment of pleasant things. *Rebecca West*

What is cricket? Something the English—not being a naturally religious people—have had to invent to give them some idea of the eternal. *Lord Mancroft*

For Allah created the English mad—the maddest of all mankind. *Rudyard Kipling*

The English nation is never so great as in adversity.
Benjamin Disraeli

The English go on living their literature without remembering it's literature. *Christopher Morley*

ON EPICURES

You will find me, whenever you want something to laugh at, in good case, fat and sleek—a true hog of Epicurus' herd. *Horace*

The epicure is most frequently a man of affairs, who has distinguished himself by talent, or played some prominent part in the world's administration, to whom care in eating and drinking is a relaxation, a hobby or an inspiration . . . He is simply 'one who cultivates a refined taste for the pleasures of the table. No more.' *A. J. A. Symons*

Twistleton Fiennes, the late Lord Saye and Seli, was a very eccentric man, and the greatest epicure of his day . . . On entering his service, John made his appearance as Fiennes was going out to dinner, and asked his new master if he had any orders. He received the following answer: 'Place two bottles of sherry by my bedside, and call me the day after tomorrow.'
Gronow

He approved the attitude of Tom Davis of Jesus who 'refused all the most valuable College livings in turn because the underground cellars of their parsonages were inadequate; lived and died in his rooms, consuming meditatively, like Mr. Tulkinghorn, a daily cobwebbed bottle of his own priceless port.'
J.N.B.R. in 'Desiderata'

Le Vaillant, a celebrated traveller, and a most distinguished gastronomist, tells us that the first time he partook of an elephant's trunk, which was served him by the Hottentots, he resolved that it should not be the last; for nothing appeared to him of a more exquisite flavour. *Sover*

'Mr. Weller,' says he, a squeezin' my hand wery hard, and whispering in my ear—'Don't mention this 'ere agin—but it's the seasoning as does it. They're all made of them noble animals,' says he, a-pointin' to a wery nice little tabby kitten, 'and I seasons 'em for beefsteak, weal, or kidney, 'cordin' to demand. And more than that,' says he, 'I can make a weal a beef-steak, or a beefsteak a kidney, or any one on 'em a mutton at a minute's notice, just as the market changes and appetites wary!' *Dickens*

. . . The gleaming silver device, part of which resembled a letter press, was now moved forward on the sideboard, and, as the screw was moved to put more and more pressure on the chopped duck car-casses in its silver cylinder, the expressed juices were caught in a porcelain bowl. Roy skilfully blended these with various wines and spices over the flickering alcohol flame of his burner. Then he added cream and brandy, almost drop by drop; from a tiny pepper mill he dusted a few grains of freshly-ground white pepper into the chocolate-coloured sauce just before this was decanted over the fillets. *Frances Parkinson Keyes*

[59]

Since eat and drink we must, if we wish to live, why not make the daily task of our meals a hobby as well? They will cost no more; they will be much more pleasant; above all, they will do us much more good. *André L. Simon*

'Madam, I have been looking for a person who disliked gravy all my life; let us swear eternal friendship.' *Sydney Smith*

The difference between gourmand and gourmet may be most obvious in eating and drinking, but it practically extends over all the actions and passions of life. *George Saintsbury*

ON EPITAPHS

In lapidary inscriptions a man is not upon oath.
Dr. Johnson

After your death you were better to have a bad epitaph than their ill report while you live. *Shakespeare*

Here lies one who meant well, tried a little, failed much; surely that may be his epitaph of which he need not be ashamed. *R. L. Stevenson*

> Under this stone, reader, survey
> Dead Sir John Vanbrugh's house of clay,
> Lie heavy on him, earth! for he
> Laid many heavy loads on thee.

A. Evans (Epitaph on the architect Sir John Vanbrugh)

> A lovely young lady I mourn in my rhymes,
> She was pleasant, good-natured, and civil (sometimes),
> Her figure was good, she had very fine eyes,
> And her talk was a mixture of foolish and wise.
> Her adorers were many, and one of them said,
> 'She waltzed rather well—it's a pity she's dead.'

G. J. Cailey

> He first deceased; she for a little tried
> To live without him; liked it not, and died.

Sir H. Wotton (on the death of Sir. A. Morton's wife)

Here lies one whose name was writ in water.

Keats' Epitaph

Mary Ann has gone to rest,
Safe at last in Abraham's breast,
Which may be nuts for Mary Ann,
But is certainly rough on Abraham.

On A Dentist

Stranger! Approach this spot with gravity!
John Brown is filling his last cavity.

As long as he lived, he was the guiding star of a brave nation, and when he died the little children cried in the streets. *J. L. Motley* (of William of Orange)

The best epitaph that a man could wish is: 'He loved hills.' *S. P. B. Mais*

Reader, pass on, nor waste your time
On bad biography or bitter rhyme,
For what I am this humble dust ensures,
And what I was is no affair of yours.

Kersey Parish Church, Suffolk

Here lies the body of Robert Lowe,
Where he's gone to, I don't know.
If to the realms of peace and love,
Farewell to happiness above!
If haply to some lower level,
I can't congratulate the Devil!

Robert Lowe, Victorian statesman (First Viscount Sherbrooke, 1811–92), composed by himself.

England his hart; his Corps the Waters have:
And that which raysd his fame, became his grave.

Richard Barnfield, 1574-1627

Here lieth the body of William Strutton, of Paddington, buried May 18, 1734, who had by his first wife 28 children, and by a second wife 17, own father to 45, grandfather to 86, great-grandfather to 97, and great-great-grandfather to 23, in all 251.

Heydon, Suffolk

Charity, wife of Gideon Bligh,
Underneath this stone doth lie;
Nought was she e'er known to do,
That her husband told her to.

Life is a jest, and all things show it,
I thought so once, and now I know it.

Thomas Gay

Here lies John Shorthose;
Sine hat, sine coat, sine breeches!
Qui fuit dum vixit
Sine rank, sine land, sine riches.

Be comforted, little dog, and know that at the Resurrection you too shall have a golden tail. Lairg, Sutherland; on a dog's grave.

[63]

Here lieth one who, if ye truly prate,
Ye pious folk, here lieth far too late.
Forgive his 'Henriade,' O God of Mercies;
Forgive his tragedies and little verses.
I will not ask forgiveness for the rest
Of what he wrote, for that was much the best.

Lessing (on Voltaire)

He lived to a hundred and one
    Sanguine and strong:
A hundred to one you do not
    Last so long.

From an Oxfordshire Church Porch

Epitaph on a Public Man
Stranger, if you desire to know
What end was his who lies below,
On far too many Chairs he sat
And died worn out by merely that.

Sir Henry Newbolt

If strongest love from death's embrace could save,
Reader, thou hadst not mus'd o'er Mary's early
grave.

Bakewell, Derbyshire

'JANE LISTER, deare childe.' Is this the shortest,
as it is one of the most eloquent of epitaphs? It is to
be found in the cloisters of Westminster.

ON EXPERIENCE

Experience is a name everyone gives to their mistakes. *Oscar Wilde*

Experience be a jewel that I have purchased at an infinite rate. *Thomas Ford*

Experience is a marvellous thing. It enables you to recognise a mistake whenever you make it again. *Saturday Evening Post*

I have been to Goodwood, backed wrong horses, lost £5; certain, however, of knowing my lesson. Wise grows the loser, merely happy the winner.
George Meredith

Do not wait for the lessons from experience; they cost the nations too dear. *O. Barrot*

Experience keeps a dear school, but fools will learn in no other. *Benjamin Franklin*

To most men, experience is like the stern lights of a ship which illumine only the track it has passed. *Samuel Taylor Coleridge*

ON GARDENING

Gardeners will be interested to know that the Government says it's the soil that's overworked.

Hudson News Letter

> I sometimes think that never blows so red
> The Rose as where some buried Cæsar bled;
> That every hyacinth the garden wears
> Dropt in her lap from some once lovely Head.
> *Edward FitzGerald*

God Almighty first planted a garden: and indeed it is the purest of human pleasures. *Bacon*

John Tradescant had in his garden at South Lambeth the Balon of Giliad tree, and Edmund Wyld Esq. had some layers of it, which grew very well at Houghton Conquest in Bedfordshire, till in the hard winter the mice killed it. *John Aubrey*

Gardener (asked for the secret of his success): 'Trowel and error.'

I value my garden more for being full of blackbirds than of cherries, and very frankly gave them fruit for their song. *Joseph Addison*

Five centuries ago William Langland wrote: 'The Englishman hath ever loved to see green things growing.' Is there any other country where the passion for gardening is so universal? *Gordon Russell*

Then walked to Whitehall, discoursing of the present fashion of gardens. . . So our business here being agreed, this is the best way only with a little mixture of statues or pots, which may be handsome, and so filled with another pot of such or such a flower or greene as the season of the year will bear. *Samuel Pepys*

The Soviet Union would unify the world with the unity of the dairyman who beats together into one several lumps of butter. True human unity, however, is more akin to that of the gardener, whose trained eye and patience can create a higher order out of the free growth of every plant in its own soil.

Salvador de Madariaga

Flowers have an expression of countenance as much as men or animals. Some seem to smile; some have a sad expression; some are pensive and diffident; others again are plain, honest and upright, like the broadfaced sunflower and the hollyhock.

Henry Ward Beecher

Heavily hangs the hollyhock,
Heavily hangs the tiger-lily.

Tennyson

My garden, with its silence and the pulses of fragrance that come and go on the airy undulations, affects me like sweet music. Care stops at the gates, and gazes at me wistfully through the bars. Among my flowers and trees, Nature takes me into her own hands, and I breathe freely as the first man.

Alexander Smith

[67]

ON GASTRONOMY

The first of all considerations is that our meals shall be fun as well as fuel. *André Simon*

Gastronomy has nothing in common with gluttony; it is its very antithesis. *Ibid*

I see no reason why we should not soon begin to challenge France's position as the premier gastronomic nation in the world. *Philip Harben*

As *cooks* Englishmen are better craftswomen than the French, and need feel no sense of inferiority at all. *Ibid*

The English have a hundred religions, but only one sauce. *Voltaire*

Wine lights up the candelabra of the mind. *Meredith*

Tell me what you eat, and I will tell you what you are . . . The destiny of nations depends upon the manner in which they eat. *Brillat–Savarin*

I prefer the gout. *Lord Derby* (after trying a South African port, specially recommended for gouty subjects).

We look forward to the day when parents, puffed with pride, will tell their envious neighbours: 'Yes, Mary is my eldest; she has just got her First in Gastronomics.' *The Isis*

He was the old buster who came down to breakfast one morning, lifted the first cover he saw, said 'Eggs! Eggs! Eggs! Damn all eggs!' in an overwrought sort of voice, and instantly legged it to France, never to return to the bosom of his family. *P. G. Wodehouse*

Most people have a foolish habit of not minding or pretending not to mind what they eat. *Dr. Johnson*

Only a genius can sparkle on water, and if he is one he doesn't try to. *Sir Seymour Hicks*

A Hungarian aristocrat, while devouring a quick lunch between trains was recognised by a boorish acquaintance.
'My dear Count! How are you?'
'Umph.'
'And how is the Countess?'
'Dead.'
'How shocking! It must be terrible for your daughter.'
'She's dead.'
'But your son—'
'Dead! Everybody's dead when I'm eating.'
Clifton Fadiman

I wouldn't call him a Commie, but if he doesn't get a cheque from Moscow every week, he's being robbed. You know the type: he signals the waiter and says: 'Comrade, take back this lousy guinea hen under glass and tell our comrade, the chef, what he can do with it.' *Billy Rose*

ON GROWING OLD

There are people who, like houses, are beautiful in dilapidation. *Logan Pearsall Smith*

Longevity is one of the more dubious rewards of virtue. *Ngaio Marsh*

Forty is the old age of youth; fifty is the youth of old age. *Victor Hugo*

Middle age: when you begin to exchange your emotions for symptoms. *Irvin S. Cobb*

It is a man's own fault, it is from want of use, if his mind grows torpid in old age. *Dr. Johnson*

A man is getting old when he walks around a puddle instead of through it. *R. C. Ferguson*

It is one of the consolations of middle-aged reformers that the good they inculcate must live after them if it is to live at all. *Saki*

In China, the 51st birthday is an occasion of great rejoicing, the 61st and 71st are progressively happier and grander; while a man able to celebrate his 81st birthday is looked upon as one specially favoured by the Gods. *Lin Yutang*

Growing old is no more than a bad habit, which a busy man has no time to form. *André Maurois*

It seems that after the age of eighty all contemporaries are friends. *Mme de Dino*

Growing old is no gradual decline, but a series of tumbles, full of sorrow, from one ledge to another. Yet when we pick ourselves up we find no bones are broken, while not unpleasing is the new terrace which stretches out unexplored before us. *Logan Pearsall Smith*

Middle age is when you start eating what is good for you instead of what you like. *Anon*

The cricketers to whom age brings golf instead of wisdom. *Bernard Shaw*

An old man gives good advice in order to console himself for no longer being in condition to set a bad example. *La Rochefoucauld*

At seventy one is no longer on the threshold of old age. One is just an old man. *W. Somerset Maugham*

A woman deserves no credit for her beauty at sixteen but beauty at sixty was her own soul's doing.
Anon

Knowledge is a comfortable and necessary retreat and shelter for us in an advanced age; and if we do not plant it when young it will give us no shade when we grow old. *Lord Chesterfield*

'. . . *le crépuscule de la jeunesse*,' as Anatole France so nicely describes what we bluntly call Middle Age.
May O'Rourke

Growing older is like going down an ever-decreasing funnel. *Alec Peterson*

From the Obituary Notice of a Centenarian.
'Until the age of sixty he consumed but one gallon of malt liquor a day; but later he began to drink plentiful which he found both agreeable to his constitution and an abiding comfort to himself.'
Quoted by Ivor Brown

Old age would be intolerable did it not arrive so gradually. *Anon*

I have no desire whatsoever that my passions should be spent; I liked my passions very much indeed. I do not want to be venerable; it seems to me a dull thing to be. *Harold Nicholson*

The truth is not that old men are fussy, but that they have learnt from experience how much the young trust to luck, until some disaster falls upon them by their own fault. At that moment, of course, they cease to be young. They, too, become anxious and careful.
Joyce Cary

Every really busy man should take a year's holiday at forty to recover physique and poise of mind.
Bernard Shaw

One grows old furtively under the watchful eyes of friends. But gradually one sees they are accomplices who condone the crime; which turns into a weakness, an indulgence, finally a boast. *William Gerhardi*

ON HAPPINESS

Give me a bed and a book and I'm happy.
                                    Logan Pearsall Smith

'What I say is, life ain't all you want, but it's all you 'ave; so 'ave it; stick a geranium in yer 'at, an' be 'appy.' *W. L. George*

Happiness is like jam—you can't spread even a little without getting some on yourself. *Anon*

Happiness springs from intense activity in congenial surroundings. *Harold Nicholson*

The only way to avoid being miserable is not to have enough leisure to wonder whether you are happy or not. *Bernard Shaw*

Happiness is a state of enjoyment, but one cannot be really happy unless one is enjoying the realities as well as the frivolities of life. *Lord Lytton*

Man is only happy so long as he can think of himself as a link in a chain, inheriting from his ancestors and planning to pass on to his descendants.
                                    Christopher Hollis

The pursuit of happiness has absorbed mankind at all times and in all places. . . . Happiness should be more than a windfall; and to obtain some knowledge of the mind and its requirements is surely to increase one's chance in the search. *Dr. Harold Dearden*

E

The truth is that happiness is the most powerful of tonics. *Herbert Spencer*

The secret of happiness is curiosity. *Norman Douglas*

Happiness grows at our own firesides, and is not to be picked in strangers' gardens. *Douglas Jerrold*

For they are not truly happy of whose happiness other folks are unaware. *Apuleius*

We are never so happy, nor so unhappy, as we suppose ourselves to be. *La Rochefoucauld*

A happy man may be a successful bishop, dog-catcher, movie actor or sausage-monger, but no happy man ever produced a first-rate piece of painting, sculpture, music or literature. *J. G. Nathan*

It is not the possession of good things which brings happiness—it is the ability to enjoy what comes. Happiness is an aptitude. *Bernard Grasset*

We act as though comfort and luxury were the chief requirements of life when all that we need to make us really happy is something to be enthusiastic about.
Charles Kingsley

The secret of happiness is to admire without desiring. And that is not happiness. *Dr. F. H. Bradley*

There is no duty we so much underrate as the duty of being happy. *R. L. Stevenson*

[74]

These evils seem to have arisen from the fact that the whole of happiness or unhappiness is dependent on this alone; on the quality of the object to which we are bound by love. . . But the love towards a thing infinite and eternal alone feeds the mind with pure joy, and it is free from all sorrow; so it is much to be desired and to be sought out with all our might.

Spinoza

Happiness is the only sanction of life; where happiness fails, existence remains a mad and lamentable experiment. *George Santayana*

Happiness is not found in self-contemplation; it is perceived only when it is reflected in another.

Dr. Johnson

Without inequality there is no joy. *Ibid*

So few of us ever learn here on earth to know the difference between Joy and Pleasure. The dead know. When will the living learn? *Frank Lloyd Wright*

Remember to live, and dare to be happy. *Goethe*

Happiness is a form of courage. *Holbrook Jackson*

If ignorance is bliss, why aren't there more happy people? *Anon*

ON HARD KNOCKS

He speaks to me as if I were a public meeting.
Queen Victoria (of Mr. Gladstone)

Mr. Kremlin himself was distinguished for ignorance, for he had only one idea—and that was wrong.
Benjamin Disraeli

This New Jersey Nero who mistakes his pinafore for a toga. *Edna Ferber* (of Alexander Woolcott)

His greatest moral fault was his ignorance of the difference between right and wrong
Languiani (of Napoleon III)

There, but for the grace of God, goes God.
Winston Churchill (of Sir Stafford Cripps)

He was the wizard of England and the blizzard of Wales. The late *Jack Jones M.P.* (of Lloyd George)

I can only remember one thing to make me laugh, it was the newspaper criticism of Hamlet, they said that Mr. Snooks played the King as if in momentary apprehension that somebody else would play the Ace.
Stevie Smith

If you are a pedestrian who has narrowly escaped death through careless driving, the recommendation is to go up to the driver and say, 'Excuse me, Madam, but I think you've dropped your L-plate.'
John Kirk Nelson

'He has spent all his life in letting down empty buckets into empty wells; and he is frittering away his age in trying to draw them up again. *Sydney Smith*

'Your personality isn't split—it's shattered into little pieces.' *Anon*

'He did his party all the harm in his power—he spoke for it.' *Professor Nichol*

The vices of honest men are the virtues of Barère.
Macaulay

Fortunately for himself[1] and for his country, he early quitted poetry. *Ibid*

I wish Adam had died with all his ribs in his body.
Boucicault

'She had, when she was angry, a tongue like a cat's which would take the skin off at a touch.'
(said of Jane Welsh Carlyle,
quoted by Peter Quennell)

His utter incapacity and his gift for the resounding phrase assured him a splendid destiny.
Georges Courtilines

'A play so loutish in its humours and so lacking in appeal to the mind that Hollywood naturally made it first choice when the filming of Shakespeare began.'
Ivor Brown (on 'The Taming of the Shrew.')

[1] Charles Montague.

[77]

'It always appears to me that Dick Barton, by almost incredible stupidity, gets himself into predicaments from which only miracles can rescue him. I am not surprised that Mr. Herbert Morrison has a fellow-feeling for him.' *Colonel Oliver Stanley, M.P.*

'Early in the afternoon, "Talkie" Williams of Torquay, the House's principal menace to both interest and relevancy, threatened to have one of his days. So did McKie, of Galloway, who takes longer to say less than any other member.'

J. P. W. Mallalieu, M.P.

He has a first-rate mind until he makes it up.

Lady Violet Bonham Carter
(of Sir Stafford Cripps)

Dr. Johnson was once walking in a garden with a friend who kept picking up snails and throwing them into the garden next door. Dr. Johnson reprimanded him, but his friend replied: 'Sir, my neighbour is a Dissenter.' 'Oh, if so, Sir Robert,' replied the Doctor, 'toss away, toss away, as hard as you can.'

'My dear sir, imagination is not, believe me, a mere capacity for failing to grasp what you have not yourself experienced.' *John Galsworthy*

Like Joe Miller's friend, the Senior Wrangler, who bowed to the audience from his box at the play because he and the King happened to enter the theatre at the same time. *Thackeray*

ON HAVING AN AIM

I find the great thing in this world is not so much where we stand as in what direction we are moving.
Oliver Wendell Holmes

To follow, without halt, one aim: there is the secret of success. *Anna Pavlova*

If you want to be cheerful, jes' set yer mind on it and do it. *Alice Hegan Rice*

Fanaticism consists in redoubling your effort when you have forgotten your aim. *George Santayana*

Properly speaking, everything depends upon a man's intentions. Where these exist, thoughts will likewise appear, and as the intentions are, so are the thoughts.
Goethe

Without some goal and some effort to reach it, no man can live. *Dostoievsky*

The test of a vocation is the love of the drudgery it involves. *Logan Pearsall Smith*

Great minds have purposes, others have wishes.
Washington Irving

The two great tragedies of life—not getting what you want and getting it. *Oscar Wilde*

The vigour of civilised societies is preserved by the widespread sense that high aims are worth while.

Alfred North Whitehead

Nothing is impossible to the man that can will. Is that necessary? That shall be. This is the only law of success. *Mirabeau*

Ambition is but Avarice on stilts and masked.

Walter Savage Landor

There is nothing else which will fix a floating life and prevent it from being tossed hither and thither like forming a habit of prompt decision. *Anon*

To win success in the business world, to become a first-class mechanic, a successful farmer, an able lawyer or doctor, means that a man has devoted his best energy and power through long years to the achievement of his ends. *Anon*

Nothing makes a man so cross as success.

Anthony Trollope

Who aimeth at the sky
Shoots higher much than he who meant a tree.

George Herbert

ON HELL

'Hell,' said the Duchess, not having spoken before.
(*Opening words of a schoolboy's novel about high society*)

Hell is other people. *J. P. Sartre*

If there is no hell, a good many preachers are obtaining money under false pretences. *'Billy' Sunday*

Self-love and the love of the world constitute hell.
Swedenborg

To preach long, loud and Damnation, is the way to be cried up. We love a man that Damns us, and we run after him to save us. *John Selden*

The most frightful idea that has ever corroded human nature, the idea of eternal punishment.
Lord Morley

A fool's Paradise is a wise man's hell. *Dr. Fuller*

My mind on pleasant subjects dwells,
Damnation and the dead.
From an old hymnal

The religion of one age is the literary entertainment of the next. *R. W. Emerson*

[81]

Men have feverishly conceived a heaven only to find it insipid, and a hell to find it ridiculous.

George Santayana

I believe in the ultimate decency of things; ay, and if I woke in hell should still believe it. *R. L. Stevenson*

It was clear in Hell that nobody had any money; it was equally clear that everyone had an abundance to spend. He would have regarded the phenomenon with a fresher amazement were it not for the fact that precisely the same inconsistency had so often bewildered him in London. *Marmaduke Dixey*

The devil is a gentleman who never goes where he is not welcome. *John A. Lincoln*

ON HORSES AND RACING

'James, take good care of the horse.' *Winfield Scott*
(His last words to his servant)

To confess that you are totally ignorant about the Horse is social suicide: you will be despised by everybody, especially the horse. *Sellar and Yeatman*

The best people have always been obsequiously horse-conscious. *Sellar and Yeatman*

'You've noticed how them that knows nothing at all about 'orses—the less they knows the better their luck —will look down the lot and spot the winner from pure fancy—the name that catches their eye as likely.'
George Moore

A race-track is a place where the windows clean the people. *Danny Thomas*

It is to Cromwell we owe the reconstruction of horse breeding by imported Arabs, followed on vigorously by that lover of beauty and refinement, Charles II, who seized Cromwell's stud within an hour of his return to England and despatched numberless agents to buy horses and mares and spent colossal sums yearly importing them. *Lady Wentworth*

Go anywhere in England where there are natural, wholesome, contented and really nice English people; and what do you always find? That the stables are the real centre of the household. *Bernard Shaw*

[83]

'Orses and dorgs is some men's fancy. They're wittles and drink to me. *Charles Dickens*

The impressions received from the race-week were not favourable. . . . Every bad face, that had ever caught wickedness from an innocent horse had its representative in the streets. *John Forster*

When I bestride him, I soar, I am a hawk: he trots the air; the earth sings when he touches it; the basest horn of his hoof is more musical than the pipe of Hermes. . . . He is pure air and fire. . . . the prince of palfreys; his neigh is like the bidding of a monarch and his countenance enforces homage. *Shakespeare*

Defoe says that there were a hundred thousand stout country-fellows in his time ready to fight to the death against popery, without knowing whether popery was a man or a horse. *William Hazlitt*

There is no secret so close as that between a rider and his horse. *R. S. Surtees*

The 'oss loves the 'ound, and I loves both. *Ibid*

ON HOSPITALITY

Hospitality consists of a little fire, a little food—and an immense quiet. *R. W. Emerson*

To do the honours of a table gracefully is one of the outlines of a well-bred man. *Lord Chesterfield*

Profusion is the charm of hospitality. Have plenty, if it be only beer. *W. M. Thackeray*

The average cooking in the average hotel for the average Englishman explains to a large extent the English bleakness and taciturnity. *Karel Capek*

He showed me his bill of fare to tempt me to dine with him. 'Foh!' said I. 'I value not your bill of fare, give me your bill of company.' *Jonathan Swift*

Kipper sur toast. (From a menu in a London restaurant)

The whole art of giving dinners, next to food, is to know how to pair. A man cares for what he eats, a woman cares for what she sits next. *Anon*

When hospitality died in England, she gave her last groan among the Yeomen of Kent. *Thomas Fuller*

Supper, she[1] used to say, was one of the four ends of man, and what the other three were she could never remember. *Lytton Strachey*

[1] Mme du Deffand.

[85]

What is the odds so long as the fire of soul is kindled at the taper of conviviality, and the wing of friendship never moults a feather! *Charles Dickens*

So to bed mighty sleepy, but with much pleasure. Reeves lying at my house, and mighty proud I am (and ought to be thankful to God Almighty) that I am able to have a spare bed for my friends. *Samuel Pepys*

The difference between praise and flattery is the same as between that hospitality that sets wine enough before the guest and that which forces him to be drunk. *Dr. Johnson*

He always kept his greatness by his charity; he loved three things—an open cellar, a full hall, and a sweating cook; he always provided for three dinners—one for himself, another for his servants, the third for the poor. *Donald Lupton*

I maintain that though you would often in the fifteenth century have heard the snobbish Roman say, in a would-be off-hand tone, 'I am dining with the Borgias to-night,' no Roman ever was able to say, 'I dined last night with the Borgias.'

Sir Max Beerbohm

Travellers say that the Eskimo is a perfect host. He never lets callers who have dropped in for the evening guess that the last few months of their stay are beginning to drag a little. *Anon*

ON HAVING A SENSE OF HUMOUR

I hate scarce smiles; I love laughing. *William Blake*

The most completely lost of all days is the one in which we have not laughed. *Chamfort*

The surest way to affront any Englishman is to suggest to him that he has no sense of humour. He would as soon have it said that he did not like dogs.
H. W. Garrod

Humour is the describing the ludicrous as it is in itself; wit is the exposing of it by comparing or contrasting it with something else. *Hazlitt*

A sense of humour is what makes you laugh at something which would make you mad if it happened to you. *Anon*

Laughter is the corrective force which prevents us from becoming cranks. *Henri Bergson*

Wit is a form of lightning calculation; humour, the exploitation of disproportion. *Russell Green*

A sense of humour keen enough to show a man his own absurdities will keep him from the commission of all sins, or nearly all, save those that are worth committing. *Samuel Butler*

[87]

The man who cannot laugh is not only fit for treason, stratagems and spoils, but his whole life is already a treason and a stratagem. *Carlyle*

'Tis a good thing to laugh at any rate; and if a straw can tickle a man, it is an instrument of happiness.
John Dryden

A well-educated sense of humour will save a woman when Religion, Training and Home Influence fail; and we may all need salvation sometimes. *Rudyard Kipling*

The laughter of Homer's gods was, in truth, not loud and open, but a titter. Not manly, not even gentlemanly; for it was directed against misfortune and deformity. . . . 'Unquenchable laughter' Homer calls it. What he means is that it was an irrepressible snigger. *H. W. Garrod*

He who laughs, lasts. *Hugh W. Phillips*

I can imagine no more comfortable frame of mind for the conduct of life than a humorous resignation.
W. Somerset Maugham

Nothing is more curious than the almost savage hostility that humour excites in those who lack it.
George Saintsbury

A joke is the shortest distance between two points of view. *Anon*

ON IDLENESS

When I feel like exercising, I just lie down till the feeling goes away. *Paul Terry*

It is impossible to enjoy idling thoroughly unless one has plenty of work to do. *Jerome K. Jerome*

Some people have a perfect genius for doing nothing, and doing it assiduously. *Haliburton*

Idleness is as necessary to good work as is activity. The man who can take hold hard and to some purpose is the man who knows how to let go. *Dr. Frank Crane*

People who throw kisses are mighty near hopelessly lazy. *Bob Hope*

Life demands to be lived. Inaction, save as a measure of recuperation between bursts of activity, is painful and dangerous to the healthy organism—in fact, it is almost impossible. Only the dying can be really idle.
H. L. Mencken

Perhaps man is the only being that can properly be called idle. *Dr. Johnson*

An inability to stay quiet, an irritable desire to act directly, is one of the most conspicuous failings of mankind. *Walter Bagehot*

Every attempt in the history of the world to establish a loafer's paradise has wound up in a dictator's hellhole. *Harold E. Stassen*

ON INNS

At a tavern there is general freedom from anxiety, you are sure of a welcome; and the more noise you make, the more trouble you give, the more good things you call for, the more welcome you are.

D. C. Maynard

The term 'Bull' as an inn sign does not, as many suppose, refer to the animal. It derives from the Latin word *bulla* or seal, and signifies that the inn was licensed under the seal of the abbey. Most of these inns flourished under their ecclesiastical patronage.

D. C. Maynard

'I have lived in Lichfield, man and boy, above eight and fifty years, and I believe have not consumed eight and fifty ounces of meat. Not in my life, sir, I have fed purely upon ale; I have ate my ale, drunk my ale, and I always sleep upon ale.' *Farquhar*

I feel a little bored,
Will someone take me to a pub? *G. K. Chesterton*

No, sir, there is nothing which has been contrived by man by which so much happiness is produced as by a good tavern or inn. *Dr. Johnson*

A tavern chair is the throne of human felicity. *Ibid*

[90]

It is difficult to realise the important part that ale took in the dietary of the Middle Ages. Ale, not coffee, was drunk at breakfast; ale, not whisky or wines, was drunk at the mid-day meal. Tea, the drink which the poorest in the land now consider a vital necessity, was then unknown. And ale was drunk at supper.

D. C. Maynard

A famous inn! The hall a very grove of dead game and dangling joints of mutton, and in one corner an illustrious larder with glass doors, developing cold fowls and noble joints, and tarts wherein the raspberry jam coyly withdrew itself, as such a precious creature should, behind a lattice work of pastry.

Charles Dickens

Xenophon gives (What more could Bacchus ask?)
All that his thirst has spared—this empty cask.

Eratosthenes Scholasticus
(tr. Humbert Wolfe)

Oh that I had in the wilderness a lodging-place of wayfaring men. *Jeremiah*

Use an Inn not as your own house, but as an Inn; not to dwell in, but to rest for such time as ye have just and needful occasion, and then to return to your own families. *From an old broadsheet*

There were thirty skittle clubs or more in London twenty-five years ago, but practically all have died out. Anyone who attempts, therefore, to reintroduce 'beer and skittles' into the grim humours and economic unpleasantness of a world that has lost its balance, deserves a pilgrimage to his doorstep and prosperity to his premises. (From *Inns of Sport*,
published by Whitbread & Co.)

ON JEALOUSY

Jealousy is the mark of a man embittered.
John Butler Yeats

In jealousy there is more self-love than love.
La Rochefoucauld

The recognised platitude is that anyone who has never felt jealousy has never felt passion. *John Yarm*

The wife who tells her husband that he really ought to take that nice blonde out one evening, and the husband who boasts about being 'civilised' about his wife's men friends are asking for trouble. It is confoundedly unflattering to have a partner who would never dream of being jealous of you. And the moment we start being smug about being civilised is the moment when the nursery, red in tooth and claw, breaks out. *Ibid*

Jealousy, at any rate, is one of the consequences of love; you may like it, or not, at pleasure; but there it is. *R. L. Stevenson*

Jealousy is an awkward homage which inferiority renders to merit. *Mme de Puisieux*

Moral indignation is jealousy with a halo. *H. G. Wells*

Versilof said once that Othello did not kill Desdemona and afterwards himself because he was jealous, but because he had been robbed of his ideal.
Dostoievsky

ON JOURNALISM

Trust in journalism. Is not every able editor a ruler of the world, being a persuader of it? *Thomas Carlyle*

The gallery in which the reporters sit in Parliament has become the fourth estate of the realm. *Macaulay*

The newspapers, sir, they are the most villainous—licentious—abominable—infernal—Not that I ever read them—no—I make it a rule never to look into a newspaper. *Sheridan* ('The Critic')

What is the difference between journalism and literature?

Oh! journalism is unreadable and literature is not read. That is all. *Oscar Wilde*

> You cannot hope to bribe or twist
> (Thank God) the British journalist.
> But seeing what the man will do,
> Unbribed, there's no occasion to.
> *Humbert Wolfe*

Skin a hard-boiled journalist and you find a thwarted idealist. *Russell Green*

Newspaper-writing is in literature what brandy is in beverages. *Barnes* (of 'The Times.')

Well, here's a secret. No writer does like writing, at least not one in a hundred, and the exception, ten to one, is a howling mediocrity. But all the same they're miserable if they don't write. *Arnold Bennett*

A leader writer is an optimist who thinks he can make you think. *John A. Lincoln*

Possible! Is anything impossible? Read the newspapers! *Duke of Wellington*

Journalism—a profession whose business it is to explain to others what it personally does not understand. *Lord Northcliffe*

This is a dull life, and the only excuse for the existence of newspapers is that they should make it less dull. *Peter Fleming*

Journalism consists largely in saying 'Lord Jones Dead' to people who never knew that Lord Jones was alive. *G. K. Chesterton*

ON LEISURE

The real problem of your leisure is how to keep other people from using it. *Anon*

It is only men who spend half their lives in offices who think that work is something to finish and then to turn your back upon, and who *need* hobbies to compensate for the unsatisfactory nature of work.
Frances Donaldson

Oh, Day, if I squander a wavelet of thee,
   A mite of my twelve-hours' treasure.
The least of thy gazes or glances,
   (Be they grants thou art bound to, or gifts above
                measure).
One of thy choices, or one of thy chances,
   (Be they tasks God imposed thee, or freaks at
              thy pleasure).
My Day, if I squander such labour or leisure,
Then shame fall on Asolo, mischief on me!
Robert Browning

Man is seldom so harmlessly occupied as when he is making money. *Dr. Johnson*

The only thing worse than having too much to do is not having enough. *Anon*

Leisure is not relaxation or distraction. It is a condition of mind. *Lord Eustace Percy*

The power that machines have given us has transformed human life; yet so little are we able to make a proper use of this power that, instead of using our machines as a means to the good life, we delegate to them the very functions of living. We live a press-the-button existence. *Dr. C. E. M. Joad*

Freedom? Yes, when the margin of human leisure and the culture of every man who works may widen with his work. And every man works with joy and self-respect in his work. *Frank Lloyd Wright*

In one way, Johnson strongly expressed his love of driving fast in a post-chaise. 'If,' said he, 'I had no duties, and no reference to futurity, I would spend my life in driving briskly in a post-chaise with a pretty woman; but she should be one that could understand me and would add something to the conversation.'
James Boswell

To achieve and practise the notion of leisure is one of the great conquests of civilisation. *Sir Ernest Barker*

Leisure, as the Greeks understood it, was not a condition of vacancy, or a time of 'vacation.' It was work and play rolled into one, and ennobled by being united. Leisure, like work, was a state of activity; but the activity was the activity of the mind, a 'cultivation' of the mind, pursued for itself and its own sake. *ibid*

I like work; it fascinates me. I can sit and look at it for hours. *Jerome K. Jerome*

[96]

If a man love the labour of any trade apart from any question of success or fame, the gods have called him.

R. L. Stevenson

So I say, somehow, if only for moments out of the twenty-four hours, achieve—or steal—a sense of leisure.

Soak. Nobody ever thought anything out in a shower bath. It's too fast and too efficient. *Don Herold*

Certainly it is a commonplace to say that conditions in modern industry—with its mechanisation, mass production, breakdown of skilled jobs into repetitive unskilled or semi-skilled operations and so on—have made it impossible for the bulk of manual workers to find in their daily work a soul-satisfying activity.

Sir George Schuster

A proportion of drudgery is tolerable, or indeed may even be desirable, as a sort of 'roughage' in our mental and spiritual diet. *Ibid*

I think one must recognise that there are two aspects in work, first the duty, as a condition of self-respect, to do a bread-winning job for oneself and one's family; secondly the opportunity to achieve happiness through creative activity. *Ibid*

It has been left to our generation to discover that you can move heaven and earth to save five minutes and then not have the faintest idea what to do with them when you have saved them. *Dr. C. E. M. Joad*

ON LIFE

Enough of this circle that swings from 'Die in order to live,' to 'Live in order to die.' *Ella K. Maillart*

Life is no brief candle to me. It is a sort of splendid torch that I have got hold of for the moment.
Bernard Shaw

Life's taxi keeps on marking up the threepences whether you are driving anywhere or only sitting still.
Lord Samuel

Life is full of happenings, some of 'em painful.
Frank Harris

Our life is an inept play with some disproportionately good acting in it. *William Gerhardi*

The most difficult lesson of life is to learn to accept the commonplace. *Anon*

The truest end of life is to know that life never ends. *William Penn*

'Life's a disease—a blinkin' oak apple! Doant myke no mistyke. An' 'uman life's a yumourous disease, and that's all the difference. Why, wot else can it be?' *John Galsworthy*

'They say life's a vale o' sorrows. Well, so 'tis, but don' du to let yourself think so. *Ibid*

A great part of life consists in contemplating what we cannot cure. *R. L. Stevenson*

'Life's awful like a lot of monkeys scramblin' for empty seats.' *Ibid*

Life is not a spectacle or a feast; it is a predicament.
George Santayana

I love life, I love it prodigiously. If I catch sight of myself in a looking-glass, I feel as if I were bringing myself a mysterious and intoxicating piece of news.
Marie Lenéru

Life is like a blanket too short. You pull it up and your toes rebel, you yank it down and shivers meander about your shoulders; but cheerful folks manage to draw their knees up and pass a very comfortable night.
Marion Howard

Yea, I have lived: never shall Fate unkind
Take what was given in that earlier hour.
Petronius Arbiter (tr. Helen Waddell)

ON LITIGATION

Litigation: a machine which you go into as a pig and come out of as a sausage. *Ambrose Bierce*

Battledore and shuttlecock's a very good game when you ain't the shuttlecock and two lawyers the the battledores, in which case it gets too excitin' to be pleasant. *Charles Dickens*

Laws are like cobwebs which may catch small flies, but let wasps and hornets break through. *Swift*

A lawyer is a gentleman who rescues your estate from your enemies and keeps it to himself.
Lord Brougham

If the Laws could speak for themselves, they would complain of the lawyers in the first place. *Lord Halifax*

'Every honest man feels as you do. But, you see, we must think of the law.' *John Galsworthy*

Woodpeckers and lawyers have long bills.
Dr. C. K. Allen

Whatever you do, never go to law; submit rather to almost any imposition; bear any oppression, rather than exhaust your spirits and your pocket in what is called a court of justice. *Sir John Willes*

I cannot exactly tell you, sir, who he is, and I would be loth to speak ill of any person who I do not know deserves it, but I am afraid he is an attorney. *Dr. Johnson*

Fools and obstinate men make rich lawyers.
Spanish Proverb

He said the defendant's counsel may be quite a nasty man and he might become dreadfully impertinent and saucy, and, no doubt, he would make a dive into my past. Of course, that gave me a decided check, because whatever women do we should not allow our past to be invaded by inquisitive man, and when those men are lawyers, who are the most cynical of their sex, then a thick veil and an opaque screen should be drawn to shield our glorious past from profane eyes. . . . The judge, too, at times I understand makes ticklish jokes, and so after arguing the whole matter with my solicitor who is a good friend I abandoned my rights and chose the nobler way, giving the case over to the gods to avenge my cause. *Marjorie Mensah*

'If the law supposes that,' said Mr. Bumble, 'the law is a ass, a idiot.' *Charles Dickens*

It is a commonplace that even rich men looked upon a law-suit as a dire misfortune, even if they gained the case; and as for a poor one—why, it was considered a miracle of justice and beneficence if a poor man who had once got into the clutches of the law escaped prison or utter ruin. *William Morris*

'No words of mine can possibly express even one hundredth part of the contempt which I feel for this court.' *Frank Harris* (when, during proceedings taken against him for libel he was warned that he was dangerously near contempt of court.)

There was once a professor of law who said to his students: 'When you're fighting a case, and if you have the law on your side hammer it into the judge.' 'But if you have neither the facts nor the law?' asked one of his listeners. 'Then hammer hell into the table,' answered the professor. *W. Somerset Maugham*

'The greater part of my official time is spent on investigating collisions between propelled vehicles, each on its own side of the road, each sounding its horn, and each stationary.' *A Lord Chief Justice*

ON LOCAL GOVERNMENT

The repugnance to the payment of rates has one very useful result; it animates local interest in local administration. *Dr. Herman Finer*

Local government must have a philosophy as well as a technique. By-laws alone will not solve our problems, but unbounded faith in ourselves can. *L. Hill*

Local government is the first line of defence thrown up by the community against our common enemies —poverty, sickness, ignorance, isolation and maladjustment. *Winifred Holtby*

In the good society the citizens are sociable and responsible without being unduly gregarious. They should be capable both of co-operative effort and of individual effort. *W. B. Curry.*

Before condemning his local council, the ratepayer might profitably ask himself if he, personally, really deserves a better government. *T. L. Hasluck*

This difference between rates and taxes is that we pay our rates in sorrow and our taxes in anger. *Anon*

There can be no true democracy where policy is dictated by experts in Whitehall and carried out willy-nilly by democratically elected local authorities.
Sir Ivor Jennings

To get the whole world out of bed
And washed and dressed and warmed and fed,
To work, and back to bed again,
Believe me, Saul, costs worlds of pain.

John Masefield

There is no division of the country which will suit all municipal functions. *Dr. W. A. Robson*

The truth is what Bryce so memorably said of party is now in a large measure true of local government. For many Englishmen who desire to do their community some service, local government is their 'political church.' *The Times*

We cannot remain strong without pride, we cannot long be proud without being given something for which to be proud. Every town has to emulate its neighbour and set about developing particular productions and special types of industry and culture.

W. R. Lethaby

All Governments are like wheelbarrows—useful instruments, but they need to be pushed.

The Bishop of Sheffield

Let the people think they Govern and they will be Governed. *William Penn*

We have a choice of uniformity and ministerial agency or of diversity and local democracy. But we cannot have, as we seem to be trying to have, both uniformity and local democracy. *W. S. Steer*

[104]

Where a local authority numbers sixty or one hundred members, and the population whom it governs numbers from a hundred thousand to a million, the direct touch is inevitably lost. *A. N. C. Shelley*

Every age has its symbol: the war-like ages had their castles, the Christian ages breathed their very life into mighty Cathedrals, the era of Liberalism created Parliaments—is that not a fine faith, which, in the twentieth century, is embodied in the Town Hall? *Dr. Herman Finer*

Here is a pretty prospect—an endless vista of free false teeth with nothing to bite. *Robert Boothby, M.P.* (commenting on the National Health Service and continued austerity).

Owing to the shortage of cooking fats in our house the custom of making roly-poly puddings has fallen into desuetude. *From a schoolboy's essay.*

Slices from the whitest and tenderest Surrey Chicken Breasts. Ready cooked in delicate jelly. Can be eaten hot or cold. These wonderful jellies of ours have won great fame. Each is freshly made each day by our own chefs, from the noblest meats and wines and calves feet. From a FORTNUM & MASON Catalogue (Pre-war).

Put the breast of duckling on a serving dish and decorate with dainty strips of cooked sliced apple, pear, orange, pineapple and a cherry. Pour the sauce over the decorated duck, stick the masterpiece into the oven for quick toasting, and serve. (From *Collier's*—U.S.A.)

As a boy I lived among men who worked in blast furnaces and steel rolling mills. I saw these men eating their breakfasts. A sample (with prices): ¾ to 1 lb of American bacon, at 4½d. to 6d. per lb; 3 Irish eggs for 2d.; ½ lb of bread, ¾d.; 1 pint of beer, 2d. (From a letter in the *Sunday Express*.)

For dinner, a Couple of Chicken boiled and a Tongue, a Leg of Mutton boiled and Capers and Batter Pudding for the first Course, Second, a couple of Ducks rosted and green Peas, some Artichokes, Tarts and Blancmange. After dinner, Almonds and Raisins, Oranges and Strawberries. Mountain and Port Wines. *Parson Woodforde, 1781*

I like to serve quail or dove with soft-cooked grits, small crisp biscuits, wild grapes or wild plum jelly, whole baby beets warmed in orange juice and butter with grated orange peel, carrot souffle, a tomato aspic salad, and a tangerine sherbert for a dessert.

Marjorie Kinnan Rawlings

I have often noticed the look of astonishment on the faces of people who think they are just eating two large mushrooms and suddenly discover that there is a nice, tasty little lamb cutlet between them. *Countess Morphy*

The banquet itself consisted of not only the most excellent usual fare, but rarities and delicacies of past seasons and distant countries, exquisite sausages, potted lampreys, strange messes from the Brazils, and others still stranger from China (edible birds' nests and sharks' fins) dressed after the latest mode of Macao. Confectionery and fruits were out of the question here; they awaited us in an adjoining, still more spacious apartment, to which we retired from the effluvia of viands and sauces. *William Beckford*

Soon after chocolate and cakes were handed, and then breakfast opened our astonished optics in another room, which consisted of hot and cold soups, meat, fish, fowls, ices, fruits, etc. (From the Russian Journal of MARTHA and CATHERINE WILMOT.)

The Hollandaise, it goes without saying, must be perfect; just holding its shape, velvety in texture; properly acid. I use the yolk of one egg, the juice of half a lemon, and a quarter of a pound of Dora's butter per person. *Marjorie Kinnan Rawlings*

At a dinner party one should eat wisely but not too well, and talk well but not too wisely.

W. Somerset Maugham

Alice ventured to taste it, and finding it very nice (it had, in fact, a sort of mixed flavour of cherry-tart, custard, pineapple, roast turkey, toffee, and hot buttered toast), she very soon finished it off.

Lewis Carroll

'How long was your last cook with you?'
'She was never with us. She was against us.'

There was dry toast and buttered toast, muffins and crumpets; hot bread and cold bread, white bread and brown bread, home-made bread and bakers' bread, wheaten bread and oaten bread; and if there be bread other than these they were there. *Anthony Trollope*

ON MONEY

To have what you want is riches; but to be able to do without is power. *George Macdonald*

'A man,' said one of the latest representatives of the Whig aristocracy,[1] 'can jog along on £40,000 a year.'
Lord David Cecil

There is now so large and so involuntary an element of altruism in the making of money, that the process is in some danger of going out of fashion. The more we make, the less of it we are allowed to keep for ourselves. *The Times*

Wife to husband: 'All right, I admit I like to spend money . . . but name one other extravagance.'

The more a man possesses over and above what he uses, the more careworn he becomes. *Bernard Shaw*

A fool and his money are soon headlines.
New York Radio

Money may be all right, but you sho' kin waste a powerful lot of time makin' it. *Negro Tramp*

Money is what you'd get on beautifully without if only other people weren't so crazy about it.
Margaret Case Harriman

[1] Lord Durham.

I don't like money actually, but it quiets my nerves.
Joe Louis

He had so much money that he could afford to look poor. *Edgar Wallace*

If you would know the value of money, go and try to borrow some; for he that goes a borrowing goes a sorrowing. *Benjamin Franklin*

When one man talks about what he does not understand to another man who doesn't understand what he says—that is currency. *Sir William Harcourt*

Well, fancy giving money to the Government!
  Might as well have put it down the drain.
Fancy giving money to the Government!
  Nobody will see the stuff again.
Sir Alan Herbert

To lose money ill is indeed often a crime; but to get it ill is a worse one, and to spend it ill worst of all.
John Ruskin

Time is money—says the vulgarest saw known to any age or people. Turn it round about and you get a precious truth—money is time. *George Gissing*

There are not many of us who find pleasure in working for the Inland Revenue. But it's long been the case that men will give their lives sooner than their money, or, rather, risk their lives, since it is seldom a man really believes he will be killed. *J. L. Hodson*

'One of the penalties of wealth, Sergeant, is that the older you grow, the more people there are in the world who would rather have you dead than alive.'

C. H. B. Kitchin

There is only one class in the community that thinks more about money than the rich, and that is the poor.

Oscar Wilde

The more a man possesses over and above what he uses the more careworn he becomes. Bernard Shaw

Have no desires and you will be the richest man in the world. Cervantes

That money talks
I'll not deny,
I heard it once:
It said 'Good-bye.'

Richard Armour

It is a socialist idea that making profits is a vice. I consider that the real vice is making losses.

Winston Churchill

In the old days a man who saved money was a miser; nowadays he's a wonder. Anon

He could not understand the simplest balance sheet and had never mastered even that elementary principle of accountancy which treats a limited company's debts as valuable possessions and its credits as crushing liabilities. Marmaduke Aixey

ON MORALITY

'Tut, tut, child,' said the Duchess. 'Everything's got a moral if only you can find it.' *Lewis Carroll*

The basis of every scandal is an immoral certainty. *Oscar Wilde*

Nothing makes one so vain as being told that one is a sinner. Conscience makes egotists of us all. *Ibid.*

For a man to pretend to understand women is bad manners; for him really to understand them is bad morals. *Henry James*

We know no spectacle so ridiculous as the British public in one of its periodical fits of morality. *Macaulay*

The love of humanity as such is instigated by violent dislike of the next-door neighbour. *Alfred North Whitehead*

Morality is the custom of one's country and the current feeling of one's peers. Cannibalism is moral in a cannibal country. *Samuel Butler*

A man's business is to specialise on the woman he loves and study her. If he really loves her, that will keep him busy for the rest of his life. *Anon*

There is an idea abroad among moral people that they should make their neighbours good. One person I have to make good: myself. But my duty to my neighbour is much more nearly expressed by saying that I have to make him happy if I may. *Rev. H. R. L. Sheppard*

Virtues are as dangerous as vices in so far as they are allowed to rule over one as authorities and not as qualities one develops oneself. *Nietzsche*

Moral education is impossible apart from the habitual vision of greatness. *Alfred North Whitehead*

In the long run what any society is to become will depend upon what it believes or disbelieves about the eternal things. *Bishop Gore*

ON NOISES

THE FOUR BEST NOISES
(1) Droning of bees.
(2) Clang of a village smithy.
(3) Voice of a fog-bound liner.
(4) Hoot of an owl.

THE FOUR WORST NOISES
(1) Irrevocable tick of a clock.
(2) Tap of blind men's walking sticks.
(3) Clink of a glass against a medicine bottle.
(4) Thud of a shilling in the gas-meter.

From a competition organised by *William Hickey* of
the *Daily Express*

The musician who invented 'Swing' ought to.
New York Times

It has been said that many well-known London streets have special noises, easily recognisable by the *cognoscenti*; for instance, that the noise peculiar to Chancery Lane is a kind of dull thud, as solicitors are struck off the Rolls.

Noise has become an essential part of this civilisation. Our nerves and our brains have been so influenced by the clangour and clatter that, though it kills us, we cannot seem to get along without it. *Anon*

Sounds are for me just as evocative as tastes, scents or any other Proustian time associations. *Lord Berners*

[114]

The whistle of a far-off train at night, the wind moaning in the chimney, rain beating on the window-panes—sounds that I used to hear as a child lying in bed—still continue, when heard in similar conditions, to evoke a pleasant sense of romance and adventure enjoyed in comfort and security. *Ibid*

I have tried noiseless machines, but they put me off; it is like typing on a steak and kidney pudding.

J. B. Priestley

You can make a frightening picture, if you want to, of the air filled with sounds, with words; of a stream of words flowing all day long. . . . *Alan Pryce-Jones*

There should be music in every house—except the one next door. *Anon*

Perhaps the most terrifying of natural noises is the love song of the spadefoot toad. It sounds like a man being choked to death. *W. E. Farbstein.*

The vague low song of London, like the distant hum of a mighty engine. *W. Somerset Maugham*

It must be admitted that in music the English know what they like, jolly bumpy tunes, of a short line of melody, and with the bleat of South Down sheep never far from their core. *Sir Osbert Sitwell*

The golden tubes of the organ, which as yet had but muttered at intervals—gleaming amongst clouds and surges of incense—threw up as from fountains unfathomable, columns of heart-shattering music . . . trumpet and echo—farewell love and farewell anguish —rang through the dreadful sanctus. *De Quincey*

I have handled a little pair of olivewood castañettas, more than a hundred years old, whose surface was was worn to satin, and whose twin cups, hardly thicker than shells, chuckled as softly as a nestful of sparrows. *Marguerite Steen*

There are things to be seen the eye has not seen, and things to be heard the ear has not heard. Exchange your present senses for others attuned to different wave-lengths and you enter a totally different world, where you might possibly meet quite different company. *W. Macneile Dixon*

Of all the sound of all bells (bells, the music nighest bordering upon heaven), most solemn and touching is the peal which rings out the old year. *Charles Lamb*

Bing Crosby sounds like everyone else thinks they sound in the bath. *Dinah Shore*

There is nothing that soothes me more after a long and maddening course of pianoforte recitals than to sit and have my teeth drilled by a finely skilled hand.
Bernard Shaw

There are, by all accounts, worse things than noises in Hell, though, to hear a neurotic townsman talking, you would not think so. *Robert Lynd*

ON OPTIMISM

An optimist is a man who marries his secretary—thinking he'll continue to dictate to her. *Anon*

The optimist says: 'Pass the cream.'
The pessimist says: 'Is there any milk left?' *Anon*

'Whinever I read in a sermon,' said Mr. Dooley, 'that th' wurruld is goin' to pot, that th' foundations iv government is threatened, that th' whole fabric iv civilised s'ciety is in danger, that humanity is on th' down grade, and morality is blink'in', that men are-re becomin' dhrunkards, an' women gamblers, an' that th' future iv the race is desthruction, I can always console mesilf with wan thought.'
'What's that?' asked Mr. Hennessey.
'It isn't so,' said Mr. Dooley. *Finley Peter Dunne*

> The year's at the spring,
> And day's at the morn;
> Morning's at seven;
> The hillside's dew-pearled:
> The lark's on the wing;
> The snail's on the thorn;
> God's in his heaven—
> All's right with the world!
>
> *Robert Browning*

'What is optimism?' said Cacambo.
'Alas!' said Candide. 'It is the passion for saying that everything is well when it is evil.' *Voltaire*

[117]

The barren optimistic sophistries
Of comfortable moles.

Matthew Arnold

The worst is not,
So long as we can say, 'This is the worst.'

Shakespeare

An optimist is a fellow who believes that whatever
happens, no matter how bad, is for the best. The
pessimist is the fellow to whom it happens. *Anon*

An optimist says his glass is half full; a pessimist
says it's half empty. *Anon*

Keep your face to the sunshine and you cannot see
the shadow. *Helen Keller*

An optimist sees an opportunity in every calamity;
a pessimist sees a calamity in every opportunity. *Anon*

An optimist thinks he knows what the world would
be like if it went the way he wants. A pessimist knows
what it will be like if it stays the way it is.

John A. Lincoln

ON PLANNING

Hell holds no fury like a planner scorned.

W. Lester Smith

One of the biggest popular fallacies of to-day is
that Planning is a panacea for all human life. It is just
the preliminary to an attempt to alleviate them—
that is all. Planning has none of the magical qualities
with which some people try to invest it. *Anon*

Sabotage—putting a planner in the works.

John A. Lincoln

Can we afford not to export experts? *Ibid*

The world-planners who are both serious and
humane might—if we believed that their methods
would succeed—be as grave a menace to culture as
those who practise more violent methods. For it must
follow from what I have already pleaded about the
value of local culture, that a world culture which was
simply a *uniform* culture would be no culture at all.
We should have a humanity de-humanised. It would be
a nightmare. *T. S. Eliot*

Things have reached a pretty pitch when the anti-
planners start planning their anti-planning. *Anon*

I don't like the word 'planning' because it is so ambiguous as to be meaningless. It lends itself so readily to loose thinking. Of course, I am for planning, for planning all the time and in all directions. . . . Community life consists essentially of planning, and the National Government must remain the supreme planner as long as there is no world authority that one day may supersede it. But what I object to emphatically is the widespread notion that if someone recommends planning he has contributed anything to conquering the evil. The demand for planning is meaningless unless it is supplemented by very specific, detailed proposals. *Gustav Stolper*

People to-day may be divided into two classes—the social promisers, and those who hope that half the promises made will be capable of fulfilment.

W. J. Blyton

An objective like 'the general welfare' has to be defined as specific quantities of specific goods—so many vegetables, so much meat, this number of shoes, neckties, collar buttons, aspirin tablets, frame houses, brick houses, steel buildings. Unless this can be done, there will not exist the primary schedule of requirements from which to calculate the plan. The general staff can tell the planner exactly how much food, clothing, ammunition, it needs for each soldier. But in time of peace, who will tell the planners for abundance what they must provide? *Walter Lippman*

You cannot have just a little State Planning any more than you can be just a little pregnant. *James S. Duncan*

The energy released by the scientists from the atomic bomb is almost paltry when compared with the human energy nullified and rendered useless by the order of the planners. *Sir Ernest Benn*

However wise a comprehensive plan may be, and however good the intentions of the Government responsible for its execution, there will always be events, domestic or foreign, outside its control.

Gustav Stolper

The conception of a planned economy is anthropomorphic, and belongs in the same category as the paintings of angels and heaven. *Professor D. F. Pegrum*

I believe that you can plan a new town but not an old country, and I have little faith either in the omnipotence of planning or the omniscience of planners. *Lord Reading*

The ever-growing popularity of the idea of 'planning' in many classes, and particularly among the intellectuals, is due more to a belief that planning is the easiest way out of the risks of individual enterprise than to any passionate Utopianism, much more to the desire to shelve a personal than to assume a collective obligation. *Douglas Jerrold*

It should never be assumed in planning that nothing is good that is not planned. Some of the best features of cities are the result of accident, and part of the object of a plan should be to preserve all good features and to avoid the stereotyped results of overplanning.

Thomas Adams

For one thing to avoid is universalised planning;
one thing to ascertain is the limits of the plannable.

T. S. Eliot

Under capitalism the business-man makes a mis-
calculation at his own risk; at worst his mistake spells
economic ruin for him. The errors of a planning
commission are paid for by the community at large.
(How many errors they commit we are never per-
mitted to learn). *Gustav Stolper*

A world self-linked, but lost the link with Heaven;
So rich in wonders, every house has seven;
So bare of beauty, every shape repels;
But free from slums and smuts and plagues and smells;
And blessed by arts unknown to history's page,
And Medicine's new gift to Man, old age.
Tides harnessed, flocks and herds no longer mated
But artificially inseminated.

Martyn Skinner

I feel that we have been planned to a standstill.

N. B. Schroeder

People cannot be planned into happiness, at any
rate above the level of happiness of contented cows.
I don't think that is what most of us want.

Geoffrey Gorer

POCKET PHILOSOPHY

Our business in this world is not to succeed, but to continue to fail in good spirits. *R. L. Stevenson*

Everything is funny that happens to somebody else. *Collie Knox*

Everyone has something to be modest about. *Anon*

Besides the noble art of getting things done, there is the noble art of leaving things undone. The wisdom of life consists in the elimination of non-essentials. On the whole, if one answers letters promptly, the result is about as bad or as good as if one had never answered them at all. If you keep most letters in your drawer for three months and then read them, you realise what a waste of time it would have been to reply. *Lin Yutang*

You can pick out actors by the glazed look that comes into their eyes when the conversation wanders away from themselves. *Michael Wilding*

The fact of progress is written plain and large on the page of history; but progress is not a law of nature. *H. A. L. Fisher*

Miracles are not rare birds. They fly in flocks, they darken the air in their multitudes. *W. Macneile Dixon*

Everybody thinks of changing humanity and nobody thinks of changing himself. *Tolstoy*

[123]

There is not much between mediocrity and talent; merely a decimal point called application. *J. Trevena*

We often forgive those who bore us, but we cannot forgive those whom we bore. *La Rochefoucauld*

A jolly good fight now and then is a salutary discipline. *Joseph Conrad*

As soon as a man acquires fairly good sense, it is said he is an old fogey. *E. W. Howe*

If you want work well done, select a busy man—the other kind has no time. *Elbert Hubbard*

The world owes all its onward impulses to men ill at ease. *W. E. Gladstone*

It is to the eccentric that we owe most of our knowledge. *Rose Macaulay*

It is in the half fools and the half wise that the greatest danger lies. *Goethe*

I never think of the future. It comes soon enough.
Albert Einstein

We are always hard on our own faults in others; we know how inexcusable they are. *I. Compton-Burnett*

It is the times that can perfect us, not us the times, and so let us all wisely acquiesce. Like the little wired marionettes, let us acquiesce in the dance.
Sir Max Beerbohm

Better be a cynic than a sentimentalist. Sentimentality is merely the jam your moral coward puts round the pills of reality. *Ethel Mannin*

The happiest man is the man who knows least about himself. *Ibid*

War-time is divided into short periods of intense fear and long periods of intense boredom. *Lord Gort*

Those who follow their nose are often led into a stink. *Cervantes*

A man travels the world over in search of what he needs and returns home to find it. *George Moore*

Success, which touches nothing that it does not vulgarise, should be its own reward. In fact, rewards of any kind are but vulgarities.
R. B. Cunninghame Graham

The best empire-builder is the colonist who has good reasons for not coming home again.
David C. Somervell

Never tell people how you are: they don't want to know. *Goethe*

It is the final test of a gentleman—his respect for those who can be of no possible service to him.
William Lyon Phelps

God does not want us to do extraordinary things: He wants us to do ordinary things extraordinarily well.
Bishop Gore

Patience is the Panacea, but where does it grow, or who can swallow it? *William Shenstone*

Crazy people with only a single idea . . . are the men who make things move; but they are not nice to talk to. *Rudyard Kipling*

Everyone has some useful purpose in life—if only to serve as a horrible example. *Anon*

In the imputation of things evil, or in putting the worst construction on things innocent, a certain type of good people may be trusted to surpass all others. *Ibid*

You should never be clever but when you cannot help it. *Fulke Greville*

The bitch fortune is still unkind to men of wit.
Cervantes

No people do more harm than those who go about doing good. *Bishop Creighton*

When a man retires and time is no longer a matter of urgent importance, his colleagues generally present him with a clock. *R. C. Sheriff*

I always prefer to believe the best of everybody; it saves so much trouble. *Rudyard Kipling*

Salvation comes to him who never ceases to strive.
Goethe

There is only one thing worse than being talked about, and that is not being talked about. *Oscar Wilde*

A little sincerity is a dangerous thing, and a great deal of it is absolutely fatal. *Ibid*

Capable persons are never liked. *Bernard Shaw*

We have all enough strength to bear the misfortunes of others. *La Rochefoucauld*

A man should never be ashamed to own that he has been in the wrong, which is but saying in other words that he is wiser to-day than he was yesterday.
Alexander Pope

When the spirits sink too low, the best cordial is to read over all the letters of one's friends.
William Shenstone

There is one word which may serve as a rule of practice for all one's life—reciprocity. *Confucius*

Humanity hates change and loves variety. It compromises in unrest. *Russell Green*

Letter received by the President of Harvard University:
'Dear Sir, Our committee, having heard that you are the country's greatest thinker, would be greatly obliged if you would send us your seven greatest thoughts.'

No martyrdom, however fine, nor satire, however splendidly bitter, has changed by a little tittle the known tendency of things. It is the times that can perfect us, not we the times, and so let all of us wisely acquiesce. *Sir Max Beerbohm*

Nothing noble can ever be performed without danger. *Montaigne*

The wicked are not always clever, nor are dictators always right. *Winston Churchill*

You'd better not go about injuring people's vanity —it's the tenderest spot they have. *August Strindberg*

Philosophy is not a mere collection of noble sentiments. . . . It is a survey of possibilities and their comparison with actualities. *Alfred North Whitehead*

It was prettily devised of Aesop, the fly sat upon the axle-tree of the chariot wheel, and said, 'What a dust do I raise.' *Bacon*

When once a people have tasted the luxury of not paying their debts, it is impossible to bring them back to the black broth of honesty. *Sydney Smith*

He who hath not a dram of folly in his mixture hath pounds of much worse matter in his composition.
Charles Lamb

A wise man will live as much within his wit as his income. *Lord Chesterfield*

There is no antidote against the opium of time.
Sir Thomas Browne

Perhaps the best thing about the future is that it only comes one day at a time. *Dean Acheson*

A materialistic world can't find its own way out.
Rev. George MacLeod

The best can never be within the reach of all.
John A. Lincoln

To profit from good advice requires more wisdom than to give it. *Churton Collins*

Apart from God every activity is merely a passing whiff of insignificance. *Alfred North Whitehead*

When a true Genius appears in the World, you may know him by this Sign, that the Dunces are all in confederacy against him. *Jonathan Swift*

Historians may lie but history cannot.
George Saintsbury

My experience has been that the time to test a true gentleman is to observe him when he is in contact with individuals of a race that is less fortunate than his own. *Booker T. Washington*

A philosopher is a man who, instead of crying over spilt milk, consoles himself with the thought that it was four-fifths water anyway. *Anon*

ON POLITICIANS

A politician is an animal that can sit on the fence while keeping both ears to the ground. *New York Times*

The present state of an M.P.'s soul is conditioned by the future state of his seat. *H. Lawrence Lowell*

I am not a politician, and my other habits are good.
Artemus Ward

A dilemma is a politician trying to save both his faces at once. *John A. Lincoln*

There is one essential point wherein a political liar differs from others of the faculty, that he ought to have but a short memory. *Swift*

To a member's wife, Nora, nobody is common, provided he's on the register. *Bernard Shaw*

Politics fill me with doubt and dizziness. *R. Buchanan*

What I want to know is how to break out of politics.
President Truman

All you will get from a group of ministers is the greatest common platitude. *Dr. Thomas Jones*

'Still, I can talk to 'im—got an open mind and hates the Gover'ment. That's the two great things.'
John Galsworthy

The world is weary of statesmen whom democracy has degraded into politicians. *Benjamin Disraeli*

From what motive but fear, I should be glad to know, have all the improvements in our constitution proceeded? *Sydney Smith*

Politicians neither love nor hate. Interest, not sentiment, directs them. *Lord Chesterfield*

Statesmen face facts; politicians distort them.
John A. Lincoln

The only man who seriously tried to raise politicians to a higher level was Guy Fawkes. *Anon*

No Government can be long secure without a formidable opposition. *Benjamin Disraeli*

But political checks will no more work of them-selves, than a bridle will direct a horse without a rider.
John Stuart Mill

In power, as in most other things, the way for Princes to keep it, is not to grasp more than their arms can well hold. *George Savile, Marquis of Halifax*

All political parties die at last of swallowing their own lies. *John Arbuthnot*

State-business is a cruel trade; good nature is a bungler in it. *George Savile, Marquis of Halifax*

Democracy is nothing magical; it is not the cloak of darkness, or the show of swiftness; it is not, in itself virtuous; to suppose that is to commit the totalitarian sin against the light. *Charles Morgan*

The larger a State is, the easier is despotism. *Turgot*

There are only two kinds of government—the good and the bad. The good has never yet existed. The bad operates on the principle of transferring the property of its opponents into the pockets of its supporters.
Dr. W. R. Inge

Our system of government is like an hour-glass; when one side's quite run out, we turn up the other and go on again. *Douglas Jerrold*

The worth of a State, in the long run, is the worth of the individuals composing it. *John Stuart Mill*

A politician need never apologise for opportunism in action, but he should always be ashamed of compromise in thought. *Walter Bagehot*

There are two things a democratic people will always find very difficult—to begin wars and to end them. *Alexis de Tocqueville*

> Political theory
> Is bogus and dreary,
> Unlovely,
> Not good,
> And untrue.
> That's why Conservatives make me see red
> And Socialists make me feel blue. *The Lancet*

[132]

ON READING

If you cannot read all your books, at any rate handle them, and, as it were, fondle them. Let them fall open where they will. Read on from the first sentence that arrests the eye. Then turn to another. Make a voyage of discovery, taking soundings of uncharted seas.
Winston Churchill

The writings of the wise are the only riches our posterity cannot squander. *Walter Savage Landor*

Reading is to the mind what exercise is to the body.
Addison

My early and invincible love of reading I would not exchange for the treasures of India. *Gibbon*

Everywhere I have sought rest and found it not, except sitting apart in a nook with a little book.
Thomas à Kempis

When I am reading a book, whether wise or silly, it seems to be alive and talking to me. *Swift*

To-day, the ordinary cultivated reader is not despised—he is merely entirely disregarded.
Pamela Hansford Johnson

He hath never fed on the dainties that are bred in a book; he hath not eat paper as it were; he hath not drunk ink; his intellect is not replenished. *Shakespeare*

There are no race of people who talk about books, or perhaps who read books, so little as literary people.
W. M. Thackeray

Reading, in its earliest stage, cannot have been remote from a magical or heiratic process and was part of a rite. *Ernest Dimnet*

In our times we read too many new books, or are oppressed by the thought of the new books which we are neglecting to read; we read many books, because we cannot know enough people; we cannot know everybody whom it would be to our benefit to know, because there are too many of them. . . . We are further embarrassed by too many periodicals, reports and privately circulated memoranda. In the endeavour to keep up with the most intelligent of these publications we may sacrifice the three permanent reasons for reading; the acquisition of wisdom, the enjoyment of art, and the pleasure of entertainment. *T. S. Eliot*

To acquire the habit of reading is to construct for yourself a refuge from almost all the miseries of life.
W. Somerset Maugham

I profess myself an indefatigable re-reader. . . . The pleasure of re-reading seems like that of spending a holiday in a place we have visited before.
Canon Anthony C. Deane

Plato is never sullen. Cervantes is never petulant. Demosthenes never comes unseasonably. Dante never stays too long. *Macaulay*

A love of books will save us from a fever, from forgetfulness, from fear, from envy, from the baser and maligner passions. *Sir William Robertson Nicoll*

So much the more I cling to that highest which need not and must not be resigned while strength is left to perceive it. . . . I believe, and proclaim my faith, that this solace will proceed increasingly from the great classics of the world; both from their own splendour and from their contact with the limitations of modern life. *Sir Ronald Storrs*

A book is like a garden carried in the pocket.
Arabian Proverb

When the spirits sink too low, the best cordial is to read all the letters of one's friends. *William Shenstone*

ON REPARTEE

A repartee is an insult with its dress suit on. *Anon*

'The head waiter was most disobliging but, of course, when I told him who I was, he gave me a table at once.'

'And who were you?'

A young man went up to the Duke of Wellington at a public function and said, 'Good afternoon, sir, Mr. Smith, I believe.'

'If you believe that,' said the Duke, 'you will believe anything.'

'I wish *I'd* said that,' said Oscar Wilde to Whistler, who had just made some epigrammatic remark. 'Never mind, Oscar, you will, you will,' was the reply.

A young author said to Wilde: 'There seems to be a conspiracy of silence about my books. What would you advise me to do?'

'Join it,' said Wilde.

'Mr. Johnson,' said I, 'I do indeed come from Scotland, but I cannot help it.'

'That, sir,' he said, 'is what a very great many of your countrymen cannot help.'

An eminent K.C., noted both for his tippling and his condescending manner, once offered, quite unnecessarily, to simplify a point for the benefit of the court. His 'It would be almost as if I were to see your Lordship coming out of a low-down public house,' drew from the exasperated judge the retort, 'Coming *in*, Mr. Blank, surely?'

A nervous New Yorker asked an astronomer if it was really possible for the atom bomb to destroy the earth.
'What if it does?' shrugged the astronomer. 'It is not as if the earth was a *major* planet.'

Defendant in a County Court action: 'As God is my judge, I did not take this money.'
Judge: 'He isn't. I am. You did.'

'A majority is always the best repartee,' said Coningsby. *Disraeli*

Repartee: an engaging new perfume—witty, expansive, lasting—a moving experience that makes imagination twinkle. *Advertisement in Harper's Bazaar*

He once nonplussed a man who said, 'I feel like a wet rag,' by asking with every appearance of interest, 'What colour?' *Richard Mallett*

I should like to have been present when the lady on being reproached for burning the candle at both ends, said: 'Why, I thought that was the very way to make both ends meet.' *W Somerset Maugham*

I   [137]

A gushing and enthusiastic lady approached a Cumberland farmer and talked with enthusiasm about the beauty of the countryside. She said 'Is it really true that you spend your life up on these snow-washed steeps, or walking amongst the mists all day long, or tramping through the bracken?' The farmer replied 'No, but dog does.'

'You must take a walk on an empty stomach,' Sydney Smith was advised by his doctor.
'Whose?' asked Sydney.

'Would you object, Mr. Smith, to bury a Dissenter?' Sydney Smith was asked by the wife of a clergyman who had refused to read the burial service over a Dissenter.
'Not bury Dissenters!' exclaimed Sydney, 'I should like to be burying them all day.'

'Whewell's forte is science,' said someone. 'Yes, and his foible is omni-science,' added Sydney.

quo. *Hesketh Pearson*

ON ROMANCE

The worst of having a romance is that it leaves you so unromantic. *Oscar Wilde*

Romance is a state midway between past and present. *Russell Green*

The desire of beauty being a fixed element in every artistic organisation, it is the addition of curiosity to this desire of beauty that constitutes the romantic temper. *Walter Pater*

'Confound Romance!' . . . And all unseen Romance brought up the nine-fifteen. . . .
                                                    Rudyard Kipling

To love oneself is the beginning of a lifelong romance. *Oscar Wilde*

Tradition wears a snowy beard, romance is always young. *J. G. Whittier*

Romance is the absence of a woman; reality her presence. *Russell Green*

This fate is the newly married sir's:
To think she's his and find he's hers.
                                                    S. H. Dewhurst

ON SATIRE

Satire is a sort of glass wherein beholders do generally discover everybody's face but their own.

Jonathan Swift

The true satirist owes no obligation to society but that of showing its individual and collective villainy, cowardice and hypocrisy. *Gilbert Cannan*

Not ten per cent of the American public understood the satire in 'Gentlemen Prefer Blondes.' The vast majority of them thought Lorelei 'rather a nice girl.'

Beverley Nichols

He that hath a satirical vein, as he maketh others afraid of his wit, so he hath need be afraid of others' memory. *Francis Bacon*

A bad satire made up of prejudice and personal feeling is a terrible thing. *Oliver Wendell Holmes*

Your satirist must be as single-minded and devoted in his research as a scientist. Like the medical student, he spends his life in the discovery of diseases. The cure he leaves to others. *Gilbert Cannan*

Satire is the last flicker of originality in a passing epoch as it faces the onroad of staleness and boredom. Freshness has gone; bitterness remains.

Alfred North Whitehead

ON TAXATION

To tax and to please, no more than to love and to be wise, is not given to men. *Edmund Burke*

Of all debts, men are least willing to pay their taxes; what a satire this is on government. *R. W. Emerson*

Taxes are the sinews of the state. *Cicero*

Included in the Roman theology was 'Genius putorii publici,' the Angel of Indirect Taxation.
F. W. H. Myers

The peace of nations cannot be secured without arms, nor arms without pay, nor pay without taxes.
Tacitus

Was it Napoleon who said that he found vices very good patriots? 'I got five million from the love of brandy, and I should be glad to know which of the virtues could pay me as much.' *R. W. Emerson*

Colbert said that the art of taxation consists in so plucking the goose as to procure the greatest quantity of feathers with the least possible amount of hissing. *W. Smart*

ON THINKING

A man seldom thinks with more earnestness of any-thing than he does of his dinner. *Dr. Johnson*

One thought fills immensity. *William Blake*

Some men manage to think with their heads only; others do it—with their stomachs—you might almost say. *Laurence Housman*

Earthworms and idiots find it easy to live without active thinking. So do too many others.

Dr. Donald Laird

Why should I disparage my parts by thinking what to say? None but dull rogues think. *Congreve*

Thought, pure and simple, is as near God as we can get; it is through this that we are linked with God.

Samuel Butler

I have asked several men what passes in their minds when they are thinking; and I never could find any man who could think for two minutes together.

Sydney Smith

An educated man gets his thinks from someone else, but an intelligent man works out his own thinks.

New Zealand Paper

A potted belief should be the outcome of a belief that is not potted. *L. Susan Stebbing*

Man is but the weakest reed in nature; but he is a thinking reed. *Pascal*

Though the world exist from thought, thought is daunted in presence of the world. *R. W. Emerson*

If men would think more, they would act less.
Lord Halifax

I remember well when the thought of the eye made me cold all over. *Charles Darwin*

Anatomise the eye; survey its structure and contrivance; and tell me, from your own feeling, if the idea of a contriver does not immediately flow in upon you with a force like that of a sensation.
Edward Hume

Thought is the universal consoler. *Chamfort.*

A delicate thought is the finest product, and, as it were, the flower of the soul. *La Bruyère*

One of the greatest pains to human nature is the pain of a new idea. *Walter Bagehot*

ON TRUTH

It is more from carelessness about truth than from intentional lying, that there is so much falsehood in the world. *Dr. Johnson*

Truth alone wounds. *Napoleon I*

I do not mind lying, but I hate inaccuracy.
Samuel Butler

There was things which he stretched, but mainly he told the truth. *Mark Twain*

An experienced, industrious, ambitious and often quite picturesque liar. *Ibid*

God offers to every man the choice between truth and repose. *R. W. Emerson*

No man has a good enough memory to make a successful liar. *Abraham Lincoln*

Truth is more easily elicited from error than confusion. *Bacon*

Truth gets well if she is run over by a locomotive, while Error dies of lockjaw if she scratches a finger.
Oliver Wendell Holmes

Say what is true and what is pleasant. Do not say what is pleasant and not true, nor what is true and not pleasant. *Manu*

You either have the capacity to apprehend the great spiritual truths, which are universal and invariable, or you haven't. If you haven't, they don't exist for you any more than colours exist for a man born blind.

J. E. Cozzens

Truth is so important that when you discover a tiny bit of it, you forget all about everything else—and all about yourself. *Katharine Mansfield*

What uncertainty doe we find in printed histories? they either treading too near on the heeles of trueth that they dare not speake plaine, or else for want of intelligence (things being antiquated) become too obscure and darke. *John Aubrey*

Men occasionally stumble over the truth, but most of them pick themselves up and hurry off as if nothing had happened. *Winston Churchill*

Not a few men have clung passionately to the hope we all share that the nearer to the truth the nearer to happiness, yet so far the fruit of the tree of knowledge seems to have added little to human felicity.

W. Macneile Dixon

Most maxim-mongers have preferred the prettiness to the justness of a thought, and the turn to the truth.

Lord Chesterfield

The number of human beings who want to see the truth is extraordinarily small. What dominates mankind is fear of the truth, unless truth is useful to them.

Amiel

Perhaps now it would be better to give up seeking for the truth, and receiving on one's head an avalanche of opinion hot as lava, discoloured as dish-water.

Virginia Woolf

Truth is not only stranger than fiction, it is much more interesting. *William Randolph Hearst*

'Witnesses fall into three classes; the liar, the damned liar and the expert.' So said a learned Judge. When his brother, a famous civil engineer, subsequently gave evidence in an engineering *cause célèbre* the Judge added a fourth class, 'My brother.'

William Charles Crocker

Those who claim final truth—lie. *John A. Lincoln*

There is no sadder sight in the world than to see a beautiful theory killed by a brutal fact. *T. H. Huxley*

ON WORDS

Spoken language is just a series of squeaks.
Alfred North Whitehead

The pleasure and excitement of words is that they are living and generating things. *Christopher Fry*

. . . words, whose oddity and beauty, whose strange parentage and exquisite aspects and rhythm make them excellent material for collectors. Man is an acquisitive animal and nearly everyone amasses and dotes upon something in addition to his grievances. *Ivor Brown*

It is astonishing what power words have over man.
Napoleon

With words we govern men. *Benjamin Disraeli*

A good voice can transform the most conventional of sermons into something like a divine revelation
Aldous Huxley

And there are too many words, there is too much about it and about, one has this horror of words—'I'll be dumb'—but no, one must not be dumb. Somebody should speak up. *Stevie Smith*

Words are the only things that last for ever.
William Hazlitt

[147]

Carlyle finally compressed his Gospel of Silence into thirty handsome octavos. *Lord Morley*

The success of language in conveying information is vastly over-rated, especially in learned circles.
Alfred North Whitehead

'I bit back the words that flew to my lips and pursed them instead.' *Woman in Police Court*

Words to-day are like the shells and ropes of sea-weed which a child brings home glistening from the beach and which in an hour have lost their lustre.
Cyril Connolly

Nothing is more mysterious than this power of using words. It is the supreme proof, above beauty, physical strength, intelligence, that a man or woman lives. *Edward Thomas*

The first duty of a man is to speak; that is his chief business in the world. *R. L. Stevenson.*

He[1] blew on his pipe, and words came tripping round him like children, like pretty little children who are perfectly drilled for the dance, or came, did he will it, treading in their precedence, like kings, gloomily. *Sir Max Beerbohm*

Broadly speaking, the short words are the best, and the old words best of all. *Winston Churchill*

A word fitly spoken is like apples **of** gold in pictures of silver. *The Book of Proverbs*

[1] Thackeray.

[148]

EPILOGUE

And now kind friends what
I have wrote
I hope you will look o'er
And not criticise as some have done
Hitherto herebefore.

> *Julia Moore* (the sweet singer of Michigan)

If I had store
By sheep and fold
I'd give you gold;
But, since I'm poor,
By crook and bell
I wish you well.

> *Ancient toast of Sussex shepherds.*

ACKNOWLEDGEMENTS

One of the greatest chores about this anthology racket is that of writing to authors and publishers requesting their permission to include copyright material. But it has its rewards as well.

I have received interesting and varied replies from several famous authors, ranging from Mr. Somerset Maugham's generous and expansive: 'Quote by all means' (for quotations from his *A Writer's Notebook*); a treasured post-card from Mr. Bernard Shaw suggesting that, if I had properly understood the law of copyright, I need not have bothered an old man by asking permission to quote such brief extracts; to a terse, but cryptic, post-card from a best-selling woman novelist: 'Sh, dearie—with book!'

I should like to record my grateful thanks to the following authors and publishers: Mr. Somerset Maugham, Mr. Bernard Shaw (whether he wants them or not!), Mr. Vyvyan Beresford Hollin for certain epigrams of Oscar Wilde, Sir Max Beerbohm, Mr. J. E. Barton, Mr. Clive Bell, Miss Stevie Smith, Mr. Joyce Carey, Mr. William Gerhardi, Mr. Herbert Read, Mr. Harold Nicolson, Dr. Herman Finer, Sir Ronald Storrs, Mr. Beverley Nichols, Sir Alan Herbert, Mr. Archibald Crawford, K.C., Sir Ernest Barker, Mr. Cyril Connolly, Mr. Hilaire Belloc, Miss Rebecca West, Mr. Desmond MacCarthy, Mr. Gustav Stolper and the Editor of *World Review*, Mr. Hesketh Pearson for an extract from *The Smith of Smiths*, Mr. Ivor Brown, Mr. Clifton Fadiman, and Messrs. Hamish Hamilton, Ltd. for an extract from *Reading I've Liked,* Mrs. Frances Parkinson Keyes, Mr. Russell Green, Miss I. Compton-Burnett, E. C. Bentley for his clerihew on John Stuart Mill, Mr. Cecil Hunt for seven epitaphs from *More Last Words,* Dr. W. R. Inge, Mr. Martyn Skinner for a quotation from *Letters to Malaya,* Mr. T. S. Eliot and Messrs. Faber & Faber for extracts from *Notes Towards the Definition of Culture,* Messrs. Constable & Co. and the executors of the late Mr. Logan Pearsall Smith for an extract from *All Trivia,* Mr. John A. Lincoln for generously giving me *carte blanche* with the epigrams from his own witty collection *Brought to Book,* Mr. Aldous Huxley and Messrs. Chatto & Windus for an extract from *Those Barren Leaves,* Miss Marguerite Steen, Messrs. Christie and Moore Ltd. for an extract from the *Letters of John Butler Yeats,* Dr. L. N. Jackson and the Editor of *The Lancet* for a poem on Committees and Mr. John Drummond for his valuable comments on the introduction.

Special thanks are also due to my wife, my son Martin and my secretary Miss Ittner, and to friends too numerous to mention individually for sending me an odd epigram or two, when they light upon it— a habit in which, I hope, they will all persevere.

If, through inadvertence, there are any omissions from this list, I should like to offer my sincere apologies to the authors and publishers concerned.